NO BULLSH*T INVESTING

IGNORE THE CRAP, FOCUS ON GREAT STOCKS,
AND WIN BIG

JEFF LUKE

CONTENTS

DISCLAIMER

Disclaimer:

The material in this book is for informational purposes only. Nothing in this book constitutes an offer or solicitation of financial advice and is not intended to provide investment, legal, tax, or other professional or financial advice.

Nothing in this book is to be construed as an offer or a recommendation to buy or sell a security. Additionally, the material in this book does not constitute a representation that the investments described herein are suitable or appropriate for any person.

Such content therefore should not be relied upon for the making of any personal financial and investment decisions. Persons accessing this information are strongly encouraged to obtain appropriate professional advice before making any investment or financial decision.

Disclosure: The author owns stock in Amazon, Berkshire Hathaway, Carmax and Waters.

Before investing, please remember to:

1. Never invest in something that you don't understand.

2. Never invest based on anyone else's opinion.

3. Ask for assistance if you need it.

QUOTE

THOSE ARE MY PRINCIPLES, AND IF YOU DON'T LIKE THEM...WELL, I HAVE OTHERS.

GROUCHO MARX

PREFACE

As soon as I finished writing my last book, I knew something was missing.

The lessons about identifying top quality companies whose stocks sell at sensible prices was on target. Yet by the time I finished final edits and published the book I knew there was something more I could share with readers. But what was it?

What was missing was the *new* and *exciting* feeling I first started investing. When you're learning a lot everything feels experimental, yet once you figure out a few basic truths about investing, picking a few stocks is not that hard; you buy a few stocks and sit back and relax, adding more to your positions as you get more cash.

But investing can be a more active process of learning by reading and watching videos. In the past few weeks I have started learning about smaller companies I had never heard of before: Bright Horizons, Stone Company and Zoom, to name a few. Finding new and exciting businesses that grabbed my curiosity made me feel like a man wandering the desert for weeks, parched and hungry, suddenly stumbling upon an ice cream truck.

Up until now I'd been content owning just a few stocks of well-established companies. And believe me, if you want to invest for the long-term, you can keep things simple like that and get perfectly good returns. Yet I realized something about myself, which is that the process of learning, listening and reading that gives me the feeling that I'm making progress in life, and progress equals happiness.

These new companies, and the excitement of finding some small companies out there that the "big boys" — the institutional investors who load up on stocks of Amazon, Apple, Disney, Microsoft, Nike, and the like — had already piled into years ago and set their stock prices sky high.

I also sense that other investors — like those reading this book — might also be looking to invest in stocks, but feel they don't know quite enough to invest. I know you can do it, and I want to help you figure out how.

The keys to "No Bullsh*t investing:

1. You don't need a financial adviser
2. You don't need a diversified portfolio
3. Look forward to stock market crashes
4. Don't pay attention to market forecasts
5. You must have cash when markets decline
6. Never confuse speculation with investing
7. Wait years for the right long-term investment

There are a lot of people out there who want to sell you on their brokerage firms, their financial advising services, or overpriced stock. As Warren Buffett[1] said, "Many commentators...are fond of saying that the small investor has no chance in a market now dominated by the erratic behavior of the big boys. This conclusion is dead wrong: Such markets are ideal for any investor - small or large - so long as he sticks to his investment knitting."

I want this book to help you identify stocks of companies, whether they're large or small, as long as they're outstanding.

Whether you're a professional or just starting out, whether you like the predictable or the exciting, you're going to learn some new tools you can use in this book. We'll dive deep into some new companies just hitting the market, as well as some older established names, and you'll soon learn how to figure out which businesses make sense, and at what price.

INTRODUCTION

A lot of the investing world is stacked against the investor who tries to pick individual stocks. If it were easy to get rich just buying stocks then everyone with some money to throw at a stock trading app would get rich.

But, as you've seen (or experienced if you've been at it a while) it's not quite as easy as you might hope from the outside. There are some decisions that investors make that hurt themselves, and other things that are just the game being set up to destroy the small investor.

The thing is, when you're just starting out, you don't know what the enemies to your success are, so you just try a little of everything, and maybe see that some things worked out, and others didn't, but aside from the adrenaline rush for being along for the crazy ride, you have no idea why some amazing ideas turned out to lose you a lot of money, and a few others you never expected to work out were your best bets.

I'm here to tell you that it's not your fault! A lot of stock investing — especially the way the cards are stacked during the recent spate of unicorn companies with their IPOs — are really set up to benefit investment bankers, venture capitalists, and company insiders. You don't even know the ways that the whole scenario is set up to pull the wool over your eyes while enticing you to buy stocks as soon as they hit the market.

Some of the heartbreaking losses you might experience early on are because of two main problems: you didn't really understand the company you bought stock in, or your emotions took over at the wrong time, and you made a decision based on emotion.

1. **Buying IPOs is usually a bad idea:** You will see why buying stocks when they first hit the market is often a big mistake. I will show you how the game is set up to fool you into paying too much when sellers decide to offer their shares to the world through initial public offerings (IPOs).

2. **How to Get Them When They're Little:** How to buy stocks of outstanding companies with talented leaders before they become huge, well-known companies that everyone knows about. I'll do a deep dive into one company in particular that recently caught my eye.

3. **How to Pay a Sensible Price:** You must learn how to determine a sensible price when buying stock: pay too much and you may never break even. We'll look at one specific stock from today's market — a company whose stock skyrocketed after the IPO. We'll figure out what stock price makes sense. I learned this method from a rare video (that I've never seen since) where Warren Buffett explained the exact method he uses, and I will share it with you.

I want to share with you the info I wish I had when I was starting out. I've learned so much from reading and direct experience, and I'm good at explaining complicated things in simple ways.

The key to investing is really simple. Don't let anyone tell you it's hard, and don't fall for the illusory picture that financial advisers, brokers, or financial media paint to make you think you need to buy their advice. It's bullsh*t.

The main thing you need is to understand companies before you buy their stock, and don't do anything stupid. This book will show you how to research a company so you become a more well-informed, confident investor.

You will also learn:

- **A simple secret:** This one trick will help you decide if a company is ridiculously overvalued. Because if you pay too much you may never break even, and it hurts to get stuck at the bottom of a deep hole when you pay too much for a stock and it just pulls you down into the muck and mire like quicksand[1]. I will teach you how to figure out if a company — and this applies especially well to tech, software, cloud computing, fintech[2] and other growth stocks — is a good buy, or if you should wait for a lower price.

- **How to use the PALMS Filtering System:** You will learn to use the simple PALMS system to help you evaluate potential stocks for investment based on **P**rofitability, **A**daptability, **L**oyalty, **M**oat & **S**ensible Price. This one section will be easy for you to remember and recall whenever you need to decide if a stock is a solid candidate for a long-term investment.

- **The Magic Box**: One of the most useful investing superpowers you can get is "The Magic Box" that I stumbled upon when I was 26 years old. I tried it out and the simple practice have helped me grow my money over many years and has made my life much better than if I'd never discovered it. I feel that more people, especially young people who are just starting out will benefit tremendously from this simple education that even a seven year old can understand. I will share the magic box with you.

I'll show you a shortcut for finding the most important items about any company when diving into an annual report, and I'll teach you how to read a 10-K so you'll have all the details you need to make smart investments.

Finally, I'll take a look at three stocks of companies that are new to me, and which you may never have heard about until now. I'll run these through the PALMS Filtering System so you can see how it's done, and you can see whether these companies pass the test.

ONE

UNICORN PIMPING

WE'VE NEVER SEEN anything like this stampede of unicorns[1]. The number of billion dollar companies to IPO in 2019 was a first, and we have no clue how this will end.

How many companies went public in just one year? Airbnb, Lyft, Uber, Pinterest, Beyond Meat, Peloton, Slack, Zoom[2], and the list goes on.

But there may be trouble underway in unicornland. Many of these companies are not making money yet. They are selling at extremely high valuations, and this party is gonna end badly.

The stock prices of unicorns probably won't remain insanely inflated forever.

IPOs tend to send stock prices to ridiculous highs fueled by the hype and confetti leading up to IPO day. There is tremendous financial incentive for companies to go public and generate huge commissions for the investment banks and advisers involved.

"The idea of saying the best place in the world I could put my money is something where all the selling incentives are there, commissions are higher, the animal spirits are rising, that that's going to better than one thousand other things I could buy where there is no similar enthusiasm ... just doesn't make any sense[3]."

WARREN BUFFETT

Unicorn Pimping

In one of Scott Galloway's YouTube videos[4] he said, "I think you're saving retail investors from a lot of pain if you point out kind of the other side of the argument as opposed to the 99% percent of the unicorn industrial complex that is there just to pimp these things."

I think most of my readers, many of whom are small investors, are being fed a lot of bullsh*t and pie-in-the-sky to make venture capital investors and company insiders rich when the stock price takes off. But once they start selling their shares, which often happens...*watch out!*

Why are there so many unicorns? Well, for one, our business climate favors the rapid creation of companies with many active users. These fast-growing tech companies like to claim their user base is enormous and growing to the sky.

Also, the powerful combination of mobile phones and cloud

computing make it easy for companies to get users quickly. Companies that would never have existed before the mobile phone, like Uber and Lyft, are now flourishing. Many unicorn companies Cloud computing is letting many of these unicorns provide fast, secure transactions in a scalable way.

Before cloud computing, companies had to invest in servers and computers gradually when money was available for new equipment, cloud computing is comparatively inexpensive and lets companies scale their business at low cost. Network effects are what many of these unicorns are after, a situation where the system grows more powerful with each new user.

This means companies are trying to outgrow one another fast er than ever before, and many do this without profits. The idea is, "let's scale this as big as we can get it, and later we can make up with it with better margins" or something like that. Growing as large as possible as fast as possible, known as "blitzscaling," and it's happening all around us in the tech world. Reid Hoffman, who co-authored a book about blitzscaling[5] said, "In a connected world, someone will build an Amazon. The only question is who and how."

Which of these companies IPOs will become among the all-time best of recent history like Google (2004), Facebook (2012) or Alibaba (2014)? And how much are you willing to risk just to play this risky game? It reminds me of the claw game where you have to play a dollar to win some spectacular prize. Yet the claw is rigged to make it extremely hard to pick up the iPhone and other eye candy. Yet people love to play the claw game, the belief that they'll get lucky and hit it big. When it comes to buying stock in a unicorn[6], the chances of winning are not so great.

The unicorn firms are looking at a combined valuation of more than a third of a trillion dollars — roughly, as it happens, the same as that which resulted from the IPOs of Google (2004), Facebook (2012), and Alibaba (2014). Those IPOs, which led to the creation of over a trillion dollars of value, were among the most successful ever and have been burned into the memory of fund managers. If you owned those shares you outperformed; if you didn't you risked being fired[7].

The current herd all seek to suggest that they offer the same sort of opportunity as Google, Facebook, and Alibaba: enormous potential markets, limited physical plant and staff, high margins, and imposing barriers to entry.

"This isn't chicken shit, it's chicken salad"

One of the key lessons I'd like to share with you in this book is that things are stacked against you (and me) as retail investors, and when I say retail I'm distinguishing between us, regular people who invest for our futures and the big institutional investors who make money in many different ways -- such as bringing companies public as investment bankers, or running hedge funds or mutual funds — jobs where they make huge salaries and commissions to pimp the stocks people like us buy.

Many readers are already familiar with Robinhood, a mobile app that has offered free stock trades since it was founded in 2013. The firm has posed a serious threat to Charles Schwab, TD Ameritrade, E-Trade and other brokerage firms. Robinhood has allowed its customers, who are mainly millennials, to trade without fees, and these free stock trades have effectively forced other brokerage firms to offer free stock and ETF trades so they don't become irrelevant to the younger generation of investors.

Robinhood is a credible threat to Schwab, Fidelity, E-trade and TD Ameritrade, and when it launches its IPO it will likely be at an insanely high stock price. Let's take a look at why the price will probably be so lofty.

Robinhood has raised $862 million in funding at a valuation of $7.6 billion and has registered an estimated $69 million in revenues last year. To keep things simple, just look at those last two numbers, what that means is that the company has taken about $70 million dollars, but it's being valued by private investors as being worth over $7 billion dollars.

Galloway, who knows a lot about private and public companies — especially about IPOs — believes Robinhood's valuation is insanely high and its future public offering[8] will likely be a disaster for small investors[9].

In a recent video[10] professor Scott Galloway,[11] who knows a lot about private and public companies, shed light on companies going public. Speaking of Robinhood's valuation compared to its comparatively meager revenues, Galloway said, "So let me get this — a hundred times revenues — so Robinhood, I think you're awesome, I think you're wonderful and you are ridiculously fucking overvalued."

Money is illusory in in the last round of valuations before a company's IPO because private investors (venture capital firms and insanely rich people) have "preferred" stock which provides them with protections that essentially cause the stock to public at a higher valuation than the price they paid when they invested.

There is so much money to be made by the venture capitalists, investment banks, and company insiders that there's a massive effort to fool everybody who's thinking of buying the stock when that it's worth the high IPO price. This is their payday, this is where billions of dollars are made instantly. Galloway explains the concerted effort to fool small investors this way:

What a lot of private investors, specifically the unicorn industrial complex have tried to do is to convince the market that, oh, in fact that number is a real number and they release that number, and act as if the company is worth that and if it's growing it must be worth more and 'hey you fucking idiot retail investors you must be willing to pay this number' and we'll hire an investment bank to get an analyst — a smart equity analyst to basically lie —and say 'this isn't chicken shit, it's chicken salad' and overestimate all the growth prospects and then try and foist it on retail investors, and if that sounds cynical, it is and it's also true.

SCOTT GALLOWAY

When something doesn't make sense

I have searched the Internet and found instances where soon after the IPO, executives of a company, from the CEO right on down to the marketing director, chief financial officer, accounting officers and legal officers for a company had sold their shares.

It's common these days for a CEO can instantly become a billionaire after the company they founded goes public, and other executives in marketing and finance sometimes become multi-millionaires worth between $15 million and $40 million — and often more — through selling the stocks they've received as compensation or bonuses.

So, if I'm going to double my money in the stock, then these executives would be worth between $30 million and $80 million. That's the chief financial officer or the chief marketing officer, mind you — not even the CEO. In my view, *something didn't make sense*. I can't put my finger on it, but it reminded me of a story Peter Lynch told[12] about an investor relations representative he met while visiting a company called Tandon.

Beware of ordinary people with fortunes

I recall an anecdote from Peter Lynch's book *One Up on Wall Street*[13] that reminded me of what's currently happening with the promotion of the Unicorn Industrial Complex.[14]

As part of his research about potential companies for investment, Lynch liked to visit company headquarters or go to annual meetings — not so much for the formal sessions, but for the informational gatherings. "Depending on how serious you want to get about this, the annual meeting is your best chance to develop useful contacts[15]."

Lynch explained how he went to see Tandon, a company he dismissed in the first place on account of its being in the hot floppy-disk industry[16]. He had an interesting encounter with the investor relations man. "He was as polite, well-scrubbed, and well-spoken as any other investor relations person. However, when I looked him up in the Tandon proxy statement (among other things, proxy statements tell you how many shares are owned by the various corporate officers and directors, and how much those people are paid), I discovered that between his Tandon stock options and direct stock purchases, this man, who had not been with the company very long, was worth about $20 million.

Somehow, that this average person was so well-off thanks to Tandon seemed too good to be true. The stock already had gone up eightfold into high p/e euphoria. Thinking about this for a minute, I realized that if Tandon doubled again, the investor relations man would be worth $40 million. For me to make money in the stock, he would hav to get twice as rich as he was already, and already he was many times richer than I figured he should be. The whole setup just wasn't realistic. There were other reasons I declined to invest, but the interview was the kicker. The stock dropped from $35 1/4 to 1 3/8, adjusted for splits.

Lynch went on to say, "I could never prove this scientifically, but if you can't imagine how a company representative could ever get that rich, chances are you're right."

TWO

GET 'EM WHEN THEY'RE LITTLE

WHAT IF INSTEAD OF buying stocks of older, more established companies with years of history we actually tried to find some little companies on their way to becoming the next big thing?

I've been thinking a lot about buying stocks of companies before the whole world knows about them, getting them early enough so they can grow enough that their stock price can double, and then quadruple, and keep growing.

Investor Charlie Munger talks about the best way to invest in big companies. "How do you get into these great companies?" he asks. "One method is what I'd call the method of finding them small, get 'em when they're little. For example, buy Wal-Mart when Sam Walton first goes public and so forth. And a lot of people try to do just that. And it's a very beguiling idea. If I were a young man, I might actually go into it[1]."

So I like the idea of investing in relatively small companies. It's much easier to grow from a small size and double your sales than when you're already an enormous company.

In my earlier books about investing I looked mainly at large, well-established companies with a long string of profitable years in the past, with barriers to entry that provide a durable competitive advantage.

Getting 'em when they're little appeals to me because enormous companies eventually hit a point where they are so big it's hard for them to grow fast. I'm talking about Amazon, Apple, Berkshire Hathaway, Disney, Nike, Starbucks, Walmart, etc. It's hard to get your money to increase 4x or 6x or 10x when you're starting from a huge base.

Once a company is huge and followed by institutional investors[2] you no longer have a chance to buy shares when the company is not well know and the stock might be cheap. Low prices can sometimes occur in small companies that are not followed by the financial analysts who work for the big brokerage firms.

For long-term investors who don't want to monitor their investments, and who prefer to just buy once and never have to think about them again, I think investing in just a few stocks of a few outstanding companies makes a lot of sense. If what you want is to just focus on large, proven companies you can skip right ahead to the chapter titled "The PALMS Filtering System," and you'll learn everything you need.

But for other investors who want to find ways to build a portfolio with the chance to grow at a faster clip. If you're young, the money you've invested in the stock market can withstand the fluctuations, and if you sit tight during declines you'll survive the gyrations and do fine.

So, for those investors who want to try to get stock returns that are several percent better than the market, I'd like to share some strategies for finding companies that can help you get there.

We are going to look at a company that went public in 2019. We'll do the deep research necessary to make a smart decision. The legendary fund manager Peter Lynch[3] said, "Investing without research is like playing stud poker and never looking at the cards. If you don't understand your investment on a fundamental, business level, then you're not actually investing at all. You're gambling. Worse yet, you're gambling blind without any logical justification for why a stock should go up."

We'll do a deep dive into Zoom now, and then later we'll look at a few other small companies to learn more about understanding the basics of companies before buying stock.

What is Zoom Video Communications?

Zoom is a video conferencing platform, built on the cloud, and heavily used for business communication. According to the S-1[4], the company's mission is to provide a full collection of products that simplify video communications.

"The cornerstone of our platform is Zoom Meetings, around which we provide a full suite of products and features designed to give users a frictionless communications experience. Users are comprised of both hosts who organize video meetings and the individual attendees who participate in those video meetings."

A few notes that caught my eye:

- Zoom's growth rate is terrific when compared to other companies in the software as a service (SaaS) category. In 2018 and 2019 the company grew revenues by 149% and 118%, respectively.
- Zoom has maintained profitability while growing: Often when companies increase revenues by more than 50% a year they are burning cash. Zoom is not.
- Many of the smaller growth companies in the cloud computing sector spend aggressively on sales and marketing and promise investors pie in the sky after they get big in a few years when they eventually become profitable. Zoom is already profitable.

Zoom is truly a rare species of unicorn[5] that has already gener-
ated net income of $7.6 million for the 2019 fiscal year[6] while
growing more than 100%. Growing fast while maintaining profitability is a rare feat, and one that makes Zoom stick out in my mind
as an outstanding company.

Why is Zoom a step ahead of the competition?

There are multiple fundamental factors that contribute to Zoom's
greatness.

- Zoom's software is easy to use. I downloaded the app to
  my iPhone and sent a link to a friend. The process took
  less than 3 minutes, and we had a high-quality video
  conference set up and ready to go.
- The software is hardware agnostic, so it doesn't matter if
  you're using an iPhone or Android phone, or connecting
  with someone on a Mac or PC. Regardless of the
  hardware, it just works.
- Businesses are one of the major Zoom users because of
  their top-notch video conferencing software called Zoom
  Meeting that is head and shoulders above the
  competition, and cheaper, too.

I was on a video conference the other day with college students,
and the people who set up the call suggested we use Skype because
that's what the college usually uses. I don't have much experience
with video calls, but it was full of glitches: we had some technical
difficulties for the first 20 minutes. I could hear and see the people at
the college, but they couldn't see me. The video quality was not very
good. I think that many people who use Skype and other video software have come to expect frustration and a low quality video image.
Zoom's goal is to remove the friction from video conferencing and
improve the quality of the streaming video. Companies who use

Zoom for the first time may rejoice when the first 20 minutes of every meeting aren't spent troubleshooting video connections. We'll see, the company is still new and in time the market will decide if it's really head and shoulders above the existing options.

Eric Yuan said that the key to the company's success has been listening to customer pain points and inventing solutions to them. He was frustrated working at Cisco's Webex because he felt the company did not do enough to solve these problems for their customers, so he left and started Zoom. Like Bezos with Amazon, any time I see a leader starting a company with the goal of obsessing about customers, my ears perk up!

Eric Yuan's Story

Zoom's CEO, Eric Yuan, has an interesting personal story[7], because he got the idea for Zoom because when he was a college freshman in China and regularly took a ten-hour train ride to visit his girlfriend (who is now his wife). He detested those rides and used to imagine other ways he could visit his girlfriend without traveling — those daydreams eventually became the basis for Zoom.

Yuan persisted to make the dream come true.

"The first time I applied for a U.S. visa, I was rejected. I continued to apply again and again over the course of two years and finally received my visa on the ninth try."

ERIC YUAN

Zoom obsesses about customers

Hearing Zoom's CEO Yuan speak reminds me of Amazon's Jeff Bezos. Though Zoom will have competition from Microsoft's Skype, Cisco's Webex, and possibly future competition from Google, Facebook, and Amazon, Yuan doesn't seem concerned. He said that he's just focusing on customers.

"I think the way for us...most of time, we do not spend it on looking at competitors, really spend time to care about the customers," Yuan said. "Really want to understand, what's the pain point from the customer's side. We want to be the first company to understand the customer's pain point, to come up with the solution, be the first one, to take care of customers. If we keep doing that customers will trust us. Ideally, you know, even our competitors do not understand the customers' pain point. Then I think we can make the customer happy, I think we'll be okay[8]."

It was not only the words, but the belief behind them that make me think Yuan is the real thing. Of course, I may be fooled and he may not be as successful as he hopes, but his obsession on putting the customer at the center of the business makes sense.

Diving in and Trying Zoom

I tried the Zoom mobile app today for the first time[9], and I was surprised how easy it was to use. Here's what I did.

1. I downloaded the Zoom app
2. I asked a friend to do the same
3. I clicked on the Zoom app and texted my friend to join the video conference. We connected in seconds.

Zoom worked instantly. The video quality was very good. I was surprised at the ease of use, and I liked how easy it was to invite people to the conference. I was as easy as texting or emailing someone *from within the app*. This is especially useful because when you've teller people you want to connect on a conference and they're waiting, every second seems like a long time. You just want to instantly connect. So leaving the app to send an email or text is not a horrible inconvenience, but it's nice that it happens on the same screen without leaving the app.

Zoom's product is a viable long-term competitor in the video conferencing space. The firm has an outstanding video conferencing product called Zoom Meeting that's head and shoulders above the rest in terms of being easy to use and reliable, and also cheaper than the competition.

It was very easy to get started because it's free to use their full-feature version for organizations to give it a try and see if it works out for them before they buy, making it easy for anybody to sample the high quality performance.

Zoom hires Chinese software engineers

One of the reasons Zoom is able to achieve profitability is they spend a smaller amount on research and development than most other software companies. Zoom has "a high concentration of research and development personnel in China[10]". One key driver for Zoom's profitability is its large engineering team in China, where average tech salary is relatively lower than in the U.S.[11]

"Our product development team is largely based in China, where personnel costs are less expensive than in many other jurisdictions," Zoom wrote in a regulatory filing.

This allows the company to tap into top engineering talent at the fraction of the cost of its competitors. Zoom spent $33 million on R&D, or just 10 percent of total revenue, which is a much smaller share than other business software makers.

I think an enormous advantage of having Eric Yuan, a CEO of Chinese descent, is that it opens up the software development beyond the US. He understands the culture and language, so he (or his team in the US) can reach out and explain exactly what they need in the programmers' native language.

Understanding Chinese culture would be another big advantage for Zoom when it comes to recruiting in China. Zoom wrote in its prospectus that Yuan's role is "critical" to the management of its engineering and general operations in China, as he spent most of his early life in China, and earned his bachelor's and master's degrees there.

The disadvantage of this situation is if for some reason Yuan is no longer CEO, or if the company is bought by another firm, then the advantage of this frictionless communication with Chinese software engineers. Maybe this is more important in the early stages of developing Zoom software inexpensively, but I would imagine that for a software company, having access to inexpensive developers at all times would be an enormous benefit.

We've now learned a considerable amount about Zoom, its product, and its CEO. That is the first step to really understanding the business. I also felt that downloading the app and trying it out gave me a tangible experience with the product that I feel improves my understanding of the business.

Now that we understand Zoom we have to figure out what price to pay for the stock. We could buy the stock right now at its current stock price and hope we're getting a price that reflects the value of the company. Another approach is to try and figure out what the entire company is worth, and then figure out the price a smart investor would pay per share. This is called stock valuation, and it's the subject of the next chapter.

THREE

PAY A SENSIBLE PRICE

ONCE YOU FIND a great company you want to make sure you don't pay too much for it. The same stock can be a bad investment at a high price and a great investment at a low price. If you pay too dearly and the declines, you may never break even, or you'll spend years of your life waiting.

It's better to be smart about determining a good price to buy and be patient enough to wait for the opportunity to buy at a price that makes sense. We will now look at Zoom's share price because we're doing a deep dive into this company now, and later in this book we'll evaluate many other companies as potential investments.

Zoom's stock price: *Not sensible*

Zoom's stock price of $82.63 makes no sense. I've looked closely at this company, its stock price, and the 22.6B market capitalization[1] at the close of the market on September 20, 2019. This is a hot tech stock and its popularity has resulted in a ridiculously high share price. Based on what I know, I would not personally buy the stock at its current price.

. . .

Even the CEO said the price is too high!

Zoom Video Communications' stock skyrocketed 72% in its trading debut, closing at $62 a share. "The price is too high," CEO Eric Yuan said in an interview with Bloomberg TV on Thursday. "Today, wow, there's a big pop. It is out of our control. We can just go back to work.[2]"

I just want you to take note of what he said, because it's the first time I've ever seen a CEO say his company's stock price is too high, and it may be the last time as well.

This is a sign of Yuan's trustworthiness, in my opinion, because many CEOs just want the stock price to go up for obvious reasons. But Yuan, who instantly made $3.2B after the Zoom IPO, was not trying to goose the stock price higher so he could become richer.

I will personally not buy the stock at $82.63[3] or anywhere in this range right now. No company is worth an infinite price, and I would wait and see if market fluctuations give an opportunity to buy at a much lower stock price.

My estimate of the value of the entire business is about $10 billion and if I divide that amount by the 282,185,665 shares outstanding[4] I find that each share is worth $34.22. That's far from the current share price of $82.63.

$10,000,000,000 ÷ 292,185,665 = $34.22 per share.

I like Zoom around $34.

Can you see the problem here?

Can see the problem here? The stock market is valuing the entire company at a much higher price. If you multiply the stock price of $82.63 by the 292,185,665 shares outstanding you find out the market capitalization, or the price the market is valuing the company based on the share price. If we do this simple math:

$82.63 x 292,185,665 = $24,143,301,498.95

...we can see that investors are valuing the company at about $24.1 billion. Take a step back and look at that picture. A tech stock that has produces one software product is given an enormous valuation by the market.

Remember, I estimate the entire company is worth $10B. The market says it's worth more than double that.

In the future the company might be worth that much, but it has to be a damn rosy future, and there are no guarantees everything will go as perfectly as investors expect.

Market fluctuations give you buying opportunities.

There's a good chance that Zoom's market price could dip down below the $80 mark sometime soon.

Will it ever get there? I have no idea. I think Zoom's stock could drop into the $70 range soon, and from there it's just a little way to the $60 range. It would still be the same outstanding company just a lot cheaper.

Many things can happen can happen during the fall and winter months to cause the stock market to plummet. Stocks of tech companies, especially fast-growing tech startups, can get whacked in a market downturn. They are especially vulnerable as investors flee "risky" stocks of smaller firms and get invested in larger companies considered to be "safe" bets. Of course this is merely emotional thinking based on short-term fears, and when investors are panicking and selling their stocks the wise investor is on the other end of those trades.

Some terrific tools

I'm going to tell you about one tool that seems like a useful one for judging the value of what you'd pay to buy stock in a tech company like Zoom.

I look at the financials that Zoom released prior to their IPO.

Their revenues (sales) for the year that ended January 31, 2019 were $330,517,000[5].

What we're going to do it compare market capitalization to revenues. Zoom is selling at $24,100,000,000 and revenues are $330,517,000 so we can say the stock is selling for 73x revenues.

In other words you're paying $73 for every $1 in sales.

Now, this might just seem like a random number without some kind of context. There are many different companies out there in the same cloud computing sector that we could use for comparison, but the problem is they may be overpriced too.

If I had to come up with a fair price for a tech company like Zoom, I'd say buying the stock at 20x revenues would be a decent price, and 15x would be a good price.

Buying the stock at 20x Revenues

You can multiply the revenues of $330 million x 20 to get an approximation of what the company could be valued at if you bought the whole thing at 20x revenues. $330 million x 20 = $6.6 billion. If we divide that total value of the entire business by the 292 million shares outstanding we get $22.60/share. That would be a sensible price for the shares. Not super cheap, but not expensive either.

Buying the stock at 15x Revenues

You can multiply the revenues of $330 x 20 to get an approximation of what the company could be valued at if you bought the whole thing at 15x revenues.$330 million x 15 = $5 billion. If we divide that total value of the entire business by the 292,185,665 shares outstanding we get $16.95/share. That would be a good price for the shares. It's kind of cheap for a tech company in a strong stock market.

Let's take a step back

There are many other ways to value the stock. No two people will determine the exact same intrinsic value of a company[6]. You don't have to be perfect or hit a precise number, but you want to come up with a range where you'd be comfortable buying the stock.

So it seems to me that want to figure out a range of prices that you would pay for the stock if you were buying it, because nailing one exact price might be hard to do in real life.

So using the example above, you might set a range where you'd buy stock valuing Zoom at between $6.6 billion and $5 billion, which works out to between $22.60 and $16.95 per share.

Now you can look at the current share price, and aim to buy it only when it enters that range. Earlier you may recall, I mentioned that the entire company could be valued at $10 billion, which would be $34 per share at the high end (valuing at the entire company at $10 billion) and $17 at the low end (valuing the entire company at $5 billion).

I would be happy buying the stock anywhere in that range (and the cheaper the better!)

As of this writing, Zoom stock would have to drop considerably in value to get to those prices. Another possibility is that when Zoom next announces revenues the number could increase considerably, and then valuation of the company (and intrinsic value of the stock on a per share basis) would also rise.

Of course, if revenues increase the stock price may shoot through higher, so if that's the case you could find yourself waiting a long time, or never buying the stock.

These are the problems that investors face. We want to buy stock, but not at an infinite price, and it's very hard to be patient and not buy stock when the price seems to be going up every day, every week, and every month.

Beware — don't be a sucker!

I believe that Zoom is a great company but its stock is currently selling at a high valuation. Of course there are investors buying the stock now at a price that values the entire company at over $20 billion! As you've seen above, there is a good argument that the entire company is only worth $5-$6 billion right now, and the market is valuing it at 24 billion. That is an *enormous* discrepancy.

There's no way to say if the people giving the high valuation are correct, or if the much lower valuation above is accurate. If the stock just keeps remains at, or climbs above $82.63 in the near future then maybe other investors see something to support this high valuation. But if you see the stock selling below $80, into the $70 or $60 range then this will indicate that maybe the stock was crazy expensive as suspected.

Beware, there are company insiders and executives who got their shares cheaply before the IPO as "bonuses" in the form of stock compensation. There are also early private investors who want huge returns on their early investments. *They want to cash in their lottery tickets. These employees and investors would love nothing more than to unload their shares when the stock price is high* rather than wait to exercise their stock options when the price could possibly drop much lower. These people want to cash in those shares at a premium, and idiot investors paying high prices makes that possible.

When those investors and insiders, who are sitting on huge paper gains start selling, you may see the share price start to drop. If the price declines in September or October of 2019 (and in the following months) you may be witnessing selling by insiders who have to wait until six months after the IPO to sell their shares.

I want to protect new investors who might be thinking of buying any of these hot IPO stocks, and make sure they know that IPOs make early investors, executives, founders, and other corporate insiders as rich as possible. Read what Warren Buffett has to say about why they may not be such a great opportunity.

"Out of thousands and thousands and thousands of businesses in the world, an IPO can't be the most attractive thing, if for no other reason than the fact that sellers have an advantage in deciding when to enter the market."

WARREN BUFFETT

Think about that — the other companies whose stock you can buy might be enduring a tough business climate, maybe they missed earnings, or maybe there is a recession or financial uncertainty in the economy.

A company planning an IPO will often wait months or years until the stock market is strong and favors high prices for stocks. It's no coincidence there are few IPOs during bear markets, and every company waits until it's all sunshine and rainbows to offer shares to the public. So keep this in mind and realize that you are likely paying a big markup if you buy the stock right after the IPO.

This is not to say that no little company is worth buying, it's just a heads-up that the prices tend to trade on the high end around the public offering, and you don't want to get burned.

By the way, I hope Zoom grows into its high valuation. I don't own the stock yet, but I believe that with Zoom, as with most stocks, with time the stock price will eventually correspond to the value of the company.

So either the stock price will come down, the company will grow its revenues and profits, or both will happen. These factors will work to benefit potential investors because they will bring the price in line with the value, and that's really what you want before you buy — to know that the price you're paying corresponds to what you're getting, and in the best case, you're getting more value for less money.

So let's say those people see this as their chance to cash in and they start to sell their shares? This could drive the price lower. Also, markets can act irrationally and news events can affect small growth stocks to a greater degree than large, established companies. So you could see Zoom stock drop 5% or 10% in a day. You should never be surprised when this happens if you invest in the volatile world of tech stocks.

As a potential investor you want to be ready. Once you have a range where you can purchase stock at a sensible price, you want to be ready to buy if and when the opportunity arises.

I'll keep my eyes on Zoom. I don't plan on buying the stock until the stock price more accurately reflects the value of the company.

Final words on Zoom

You just have to wake and smell the ayahuasca and figure out what's really going on and not believe the news media who is spoon-fed a highlight reel of these unicorn companies by investment banks who pay equity analysts to lie and make it sound like these stocks can only go up — and then they try to get small investors so excited they feel they must buy the IPO du jour, from Airbnb to zoom[7].

Here's a great quote to keep in mind:

It's not given to human beings to have such talent that they can just know everything about everything all the time. But it is given to human beings who work hard at at — who look and sift the world for a mispriced bet — that they can occasionally find one.

CHARLIE MUNGER

That's what you're looking for - a mispriced bet. And not in in the direction where you're paying too much for it! You want to get a bargain for a great company. That's not easy to find, especially among the over-loved tech darlings like Zoom.

I think the one thing going for Zoom is that it's not a popular name outside of the investing community. Because it's mainly used by enterprise customers (i.e. big corporations) the name is known mostly by tech investors and institutional investors on Wall Street. That's still a large group of very smart investors, but the company could grow a lot in the next several years and increase its revenues from the millions to the billions. That is one thing that has to go well for the company, and it's partially under their control. The stock price is entirely out of the company's control, as well as yours, as a retail investor.

But it is possible, and I'm going to help you hang in there and try to figure out when the mispricing can work in your favor.

Above you'll recall that at $82.63 stock price, with 292,000,000 shares outstanding, Zoom's market cap was $24 billion.

Well, let's look at that again. If Zoom stock drops a lot, let's say it drops $12, then at $70.00 is it a good deal? $70.00 x 292,000,000 shares outstanding = $20.4 billion

Let's see what happens if the stock ever gets to $65.00 x 292,000,000 = $19 billion.

In my view, given the company's most recent financials, the company is not worth $19 billion. My best guess would be a range around $10 billion. You can't pay the current market price, or any price near it and consider that a rational thing to do. The number is just wrong, and you will overpay and regret it when the price drops a lot. Remember, the common condition in markets is ignorance and stupidity. Most people are wrong about stock prices most of the time. That's not a cheery thought, but it's true.

So, if you want to be better than the other investors, if you want to drive your own car instead of just passively taking the easy rout and riding the bus, ask yourself how patient you can be, and when you can buy that stock at a sensible price.

Could Zoom make sense at $60 if the price ever fell that far?

How about at $50? Well, if it got to $40 a share I'd start to look more closely at the stock.

For a company making one software product (and having no other sources of revenue) I think $10 billion for the entire company makes sense when you consider the company had $300,000,000 in revenues, and it seems to be growing at a fast clip.

$$10,000,000,000 \div 292,000,000 = \$34.25 \text{ /share}$$

Nobody knows for sure what the correct price is in the heat of all the day-to-day trading. In the short term stock prices and their underlying values can diverge wildly, but eventually they tend to converge.

A tale of two tennis racquet stringers

Yesterday I went to get my tennis racquet strung at a local store. Most of these places charge you about $50 to get your racquet strung...it's one of tennis' dirty little secrets[8]: the fact that if you play a lot you will break strings frequently, and it costs an arm and a leg to get your string replaced.

Anyways, if you bring your own tennis racquet string it greatly reduces the cost of a string job. Well, when I called they told me it cost $23 to get my racquet strung. When I arrived yesterday I was told it was $25. The owner told me, "we've been getting that all year." I say this because it proved he was just trying to get as much as he could, and the pricing is not fixed, but that "people who need their racquets strung are stupid enough to pay this amount, and if we can get it we'll take it."[9] He's got a good point, too, because many people who play tennis are made of money, and they'll pay any quoted price for shirts, shorts, racquets, etc.

I decided it wasn't a good deal. I walked out the door without getting my racquets strung there, and explained it was because I had been quoted a lower price a short while ago on the phone, and didn't accept the "market price" the owner figured I was likely to pay — because hey, I needed those two racquets strung!

I'm not knocking the guy, he was just trying to get paid as much as he could. That's the free market economy, and I applaud him! But as a buyer, I don't have to pay it. And that's the lesson I want to share with you.

You don't have to pay insane prices — for tennis racquet stringing, or for stocks) — "just because everyone else is."

I didn't realize I was doing it at the time I walked out of the store, but I refused to pay the market price. I actually thought I might be able to get a more reasonable price for tennis racquet stringing elsewhere.

Mr. Market: The imaginary man

When you see a stock priced at some insanely high price, just keep in mind how Warren Buffett compared the market to an emotionally unstable guy who shouts out prices every day. "This imaginary person out there - Mr. Market - is a kind of drunken psycho. Some days he gets very enthused and some days he gets very depressed."

> Mr. Market has another endearing characteristic: He doesn't mind being ignored. If his quotation is uninteresting to you today, he will be back with a new one tomorrow. Transactions are strictly at your option. Under these conditions, the more manic-depressive his behavior, the better for you.[10]
>
> WARREN BUFFETT

So when I politely declined paying the lofty price at the tennis store, the owner didn't chase me out. He was like Mr. Market, offering his best price. I was free to take it or leave it. So, I made a call to another shop. They said they charge $15 to string my racquet — a

40% discount from the earlier price quote. I got a big savings by waiting and making one phone call.

The moral of this story is that the first quote you get is often not the best. A little research and patience can pay off and save you a lot of money. As Benjamin Franklin said, "Be careful of small costs, a small link sinks a great ship."

The no bullsh*t approach I want you to absorb is that most of the time stocks are over priced. If you pay a fair price for a stock you'll likely do okay, but when you start paying ridiculously high prices for stocks you might lose big time. Just say no to these high prices.

I believe that it's enough to own just three to five stocks of outstanding companies...but what if I'm wrong? It's possible that you could make a mistake. Also, if you buy stocks of companies that are already well-established — Apple, Coke, Facebook, McDonald's, Starbucks — you might have missed owning them during their rapid growth phase. It is possible that only three to five stocks of great companies is enough for anyone. But if you make a mistake you might be open to losing a lot of money. So the quality of the stocks matters.

Humans mostly, as we go about life, we're very selective in the evidence we let seep into us, and we like to observe the evidence that confirms our pre-existing beliefs.

JEFF BEZOS

It's possible that my pre-existing belief is the best way to invest is in a few outstanding companies. But what if that's wrong? What about investing in more than five companies? How about more than that, and what if the companies are smaller and younger, and have a chance to explode their growth?

It's much harder for a massive company — one with a market capitalization of $300 billion, $500 billion, or $800 billion to double in size. But what about a company that's only valued at $10 billion? It could double, and then double again, and double again, and it would be a $80 billion company.

Maybe I've been holding onto my pre-existing belief with a mighty grip, and the secret to great investing, truly market-beating investing, is not to focus on a few outstanding, well-established companies — but instead identifying some smaller companies before they hit it big. It's time to re-examine my pre-existing beliefs about how to put together a stock portfolio that could provide for faster growth.

FOUR

DESIGN A STOCK PORTFOLIO

HOW YOU SET up your portfolio depends on your own personality and attitude about investing. One thing I've noticed is that every investor has a strong opinion about the best way to invest, and they're not shy when it comes to telling you the perfect way to invest.

I'd like to tell you that I have changed my mind, to some extent, as I've gained experience as an investor. I share this because you might get some useful ideas about investing.

My investing life is comprised of three stages:

1. During the first stage of my investing life I invested in mutual funds. I knew nothing about investing in stocks, but knew I wanted to have money compounding in value over time, so I put some money every month into a mutual fund. It was the best investing program I could have ever wanted. Naturally I got some brighter ideas (that worked less well, read on!)

2. The second stage began after I'd invested in mutual funds for about 10 years. I decided to take a chunk of my mutual fund account (it was invested in the S&P 500

index fund), sell it, and invest in two stocks: Leucadia
National Corporation and White Mountains Insurance
Group. You know the expression, "Go big or go home?"
Well, I went big, and I went *big and stupid*. I did not
chose great companies with predictable profits. Instead I
chose companies that had done great in the past, but
started struggling as soon as I bought their stocks. I did
not lose money, but their stock prices went nowhere after
10 years. If I had just left the index fund alone I would
have done really great during that decade. I thought I
understood those two companies well when I invested,
but I was kidding myself: I hadn't understood how
dependent they were on leadership being smart, and
unfortunately their leaderships made some dumb
decisions and bad investments.

3. In the third stage of my investing career (where I am now)
I have done a much better job to learn about companies
before I invest. I'm concentrated in four stocks: Amazon,
Berkshire Hathaway, Carmax and Waters, with dribs and
drabs of another stock that I got in a spinoff and never
bothered to sell.

I believe in concentration

Some people would surely question why I only own a few stocks.
Financial advisers especially tell you that you should be diversified in
many different stocks. The reason is simple: I learn from smart
investors like Warren Buffett and Charlie Munger, and I learned
from them to concentrate my best ideas in the stock of a few companies. I can see from their own record the outstanding results that
come from making a few great decisions in the stocks you buy. You
don't have to know about a million different things, you only have to
be right about a few stocks.

Buffett and Munger say that diversification is essentially insurance for when you don't know what you're doing. If you can identify

three great companies, why would you put more money into your 10th, or 20th, or 50th best idea? Yet that is what most investors and money managers do when they diversify — they take a shotgun approach to investing in a bit of everything, and as a result they get average returns. Their returns mirror the overall stock market because *they are the market.*

So, my stocks are concentrated in a few companies that I know well, and I don't have to think about selling this company or that because it missed earnings. Companies like Amazon, Berkshire Hathaway, Carmax, and Waters are going to be around for a long time. I sit back and let them grow, confident in their long-term prospects for success.

I'm re-thinking my approach

Just because I have a concentrated portfolio doesn't mean it's a good idea, or the brightest idea. Some people would say I should diversify. Others might say now is a good time to sell stocks and raise cash because of uncertainty about the future...all bullsh*t reasons to change an investment plan that's working well. Sometimes people are their own worst enemies, trying to perfect a system that's doing quite well, and int the process screwing everything up. If you don't think it's possible, refer to #2 above — selling my S&P 500 index fund shares to buy two stocks that went nowhere for a decade!

I think there is a better approach to investing, and I'm likely going to give it a try in the years ahead. I will continue to hold the shares in the five companies I currently own, but I will invest in some new, smaller companies.

Why make the change? What's the improvement?

I've been reading three different people lately who have shaped my thinking about investing, and when I put together their approaches I see something new and experimental, and my curiosity to try this out is driving my new way of thinking.

- *The first influence* on my new investing approach is Charlie Munger, and as you read in an earlier chapter, he floated the idea to "Get 'em when they're little[1]" and that appeals to me. I'm thinking to set up an account just to invest in these smaller companies. Munger's idea nudged me away from my long-held idea of just sticking to a few huge, successful businesses as my main stock holdings. Once a company is huge (like Berkshire Hathaway at $500 billion or Amazon at $875 billion) it gets hard to grow fast. I'm not saying it won't happen (as a shareholder, I certainly hope it will), but it's a law of the investing world that once companies get really big their growth slows.

- *The second influence* is Jeff Bezos, who said, "People who are right a lot, change their mind a lot[2]. That may be easier said than done, because most people just seek out information to bolster their current beliefs and tune out opposing opinions," he said. "People who are right seek to disconfirm their most profoundly held convictions, which is very unnatural for humans," he said. "Humans mostly, as we go about life, we're very selective in the evidence we let seep into us, and we like to observe the evidence that confirms our pre-existing beliefs. Having the ability to see multiple viewpoints and understand the bigger picture, rather than being too confined to your own beliefs, increases your chances of being right," he said.

- *The third influence* is Peter Lynch[3], and I have learned most about his success by seeing how he invested the Fidelity Magellan portfolio. He is most successful fund manager of all time, yet he doubled the return of the S&P 500 (an incredible feat) holding about 1,200 stocks at a time. So, he did not believe in concentrating in just a few companies, and he could not because of the sheer amount of money he had to invest (Magellan was a huge fund).

Lynch was very good at identifying companies that were small and not necessarily followed by all of the analysts and institutional investors on Wall Street, and getting stocks that he called "two baggers" (they doubled) or "four baggers" (quadrupled) right on up to "ten baggers" and beyond. He was a master of finding companies when they were small. His record was *not* the buy and hold method, but but instead he rotated in and out of companies, and he held them as long as he thought their investment "story" was positive, but he would sell and replace companies when he found other companies with better prospects.

I'm beginning to think that makes for a more exciting approach to investing, and if it's done with a variety of different kinds of stocks the risk of any one stock imploding is diminished by the others. The key is that on average, the portfolio of stocks is delivering two to three percent more than the average stock. This is no small feat, for sure, but it's worth a shot and an investor can potentially get a a few, or several percent return over the market average if things work out.

When you experiment you don't know what will happen, and I think that is part of the fun of investing. I'm not saying emotions should drive your process, but I realize that there is excitement on trying something new where you don't know the results ahead of time. You could buy the stock and it goes straight up, or it instantly crater and you lose most (or all) of your investment. Maybe it goes up and down, taking you for a roller coaster ride. I believe the curiosity that leads us to discover new companies and dive into learning about them may stimulate creative parts of the brain that are curious to learn new things and seek new experiences, and the process of thinking and weighing and making an intelligent speculation is a creative endeavor.

I draw some of my inspiration from Ben Graham, who said that investing should be experimental, new, and exciting[4]. There is an awakening in the mind when old ways of thinking are challenged, and you open yourself up to accept new ideas.

One area where I think we are especially distinctive is failure. I believe we are the best place in the world to fail (we have plenty of practice!), and failure and invention are inseparable twins. To invent you have to experiment, and if you know in advance that it's going to work, it's not an experiment[5].

JEFF BEZOS

Benjamin Graham[6] applies this experimental approach when he explains how your investing can possess aspects of experimentation. He says you transform speculation into investment when you diversify into separate "intelligent speculations." In other words, if you invest in many different potentially risky things, you decrease the risk of one of those stocks tanking. You can be smart about your bets if you're willing to make several; you transform these separate intelligent speculations by the simple device of diversification.

Graham said that it's a mistake to think your speculation has been unwise if you lose money at it, and he says, "That sounds like an obvious conclusion, but actually it is not true at all," he said. "A speculation is unwise only if it is made on insufficient study and by poor judgment."

In other words, it's not a mistake because you lost money. It's a mistake if you did something stupid because you didn't understand the company and made a bad decision.

I notice how smart people can express essentially the same ideas about making experiments, event though they never met and lived in different centuries. You'll recall above how Jeff Bezos, said "To invent you have to experiment, and if you know in advance that it's going to work, it's not an experiment." Well, Ben Graham echoed similar thoughts in the prior century:

In some cases the thing will work out badly. But that is simply part of the game. If it was bound to work out rightly, it wouldn't be a speculation at all, and there wouldn't be the opportunities of profit that inhere in sound speculation.

BEN GRAHAM

Bezos and Graham both suggest that whether you're inventing or investing you must experiment to open the door to new inventions and opportunities. Things possibly working out badly is a risk you take so that some things may work out spectacularly.

So, I think you should be reassured in knowing that talented people like Graham, and later Bezos, suggest that it's okay to experiment, and not only that, but you should be encouraged to do so, as long as you use good judgement.

As you think about stocks you'd like to buy I hope you will start keeping track of these companies. Write them down in a list on your computer, or in your phone, or on a good old piece of paper. However you keep track of these companies, I want you to keep that list handy because in the next few chapters you'll be asking yourself five questions about that company while using the PALMS Filtering System. This tool will help you pick stocks of outstanding companies and help you to arrive at a sensible price for each one.

FIVE

THE PALMS FILTERING SYSTEM

THE PALMS FILTERING SYSTEM is a simple checklist to make sure you pay attention to important investing concepts.

Before you buy any stock ask yourself:

Profitable - Is the company profitable?

Adaptable - Is the company adapting to changing technology?

Loyal Customers - Are customers devoted to the company's brand?

Moat to Protect - Does the company possess a durable competitive advantage that acts as a barrier to entry?

Sensible Price - Is the stock selling at a price that makes sense?

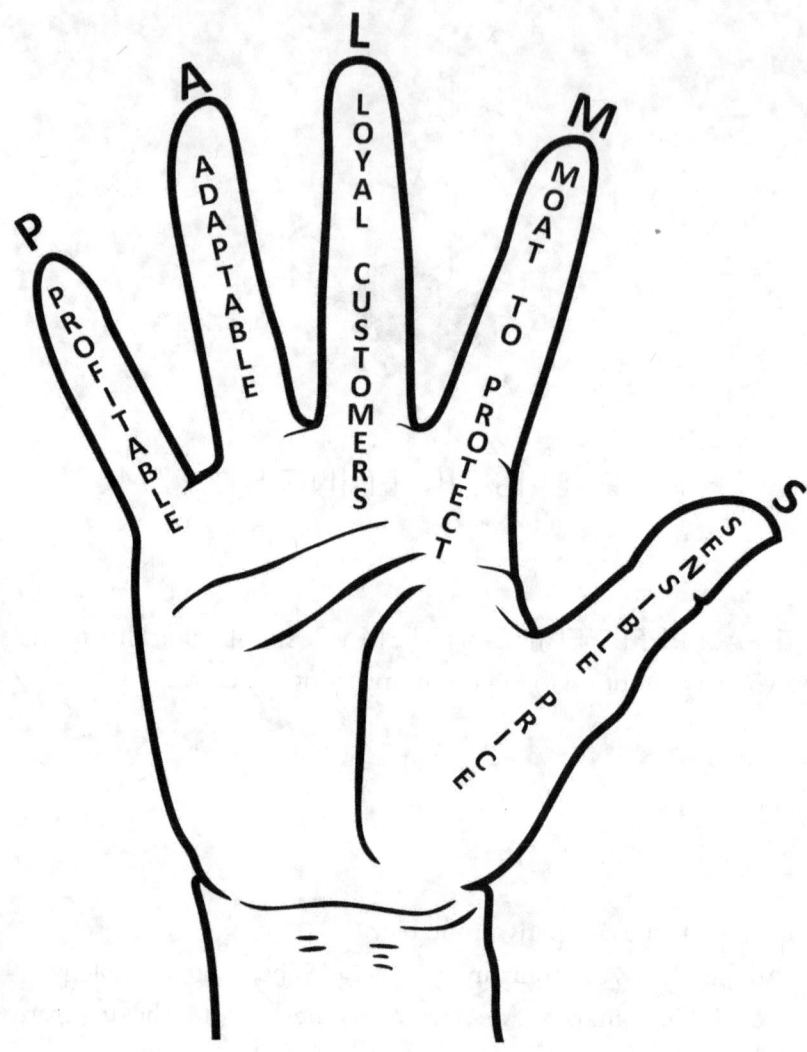

SIX

P - PROFITABLE

I WILL ONLY INVEST in companies that make a profit. It's the only way to go. If you want to go for Uber, Tesla, Lyft, Beyond Meat or a host of other companies, you start taking part in a speculation that things will eventually change and the company will start to make a profit.

While that *can* happen, I just think that hoping it will happen is not a good approach. Why sit around hoping that a company will survive and prosper when there are already companies *making that happen?*

Earlier in this book we discussed a rarity in the current environment, a tech stock that just had an IPO and the business is making money. That particular stock is not under anyone's radar, it is hot and people are excited to own a tech stock that could soar. The problem is there is so much love for Zoom that its price is insanely high.

But there are other profitable companies in the world, and we're going to take a look at them so we can start getting better at figuring out which companies are profitable.

. . .

How to find out if a company is profitable:

Determining profitability is easy to do, but you have to know where to look. If you take an accounting class it's one of the first things you'll probably learn about, but for those readers who never took accounting I'll show you what you need to know.

As a heads-up, we'll go into much more detail later in the book in where we'll learn how to read an annual report which includes all the useful numbers that you need to know.

But for now you don't have to have an in-depth skills in reading the annual report. You just need to download the annual report and find the useful page.

Let's say you were thinking of investing in Costco. A quick online search for "Costco Annual Report" will bring you to a page with annual reports going back to 1998!

Here's the cover of Costco's most recent annual report:

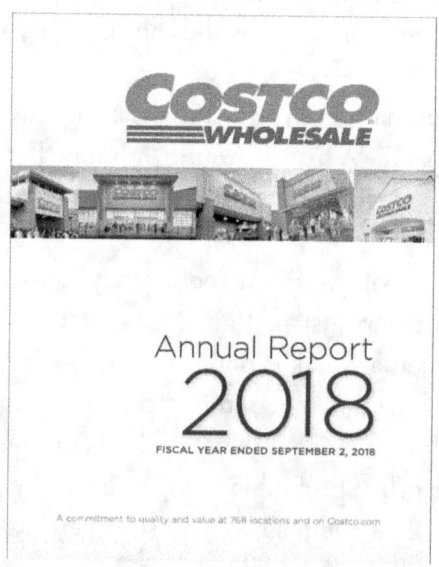

Scroll and look for "Selected Financial Data" to find this:

Item 6—Selected Financial Data

The following table sets forth information concerning our consolidated financial condition, operating results, and key operating metrics. This information should be read in conjunction with Management's Discussion and Analysis of Financial Condition and Results of Operations, included in Item 7 of this Report, and our consolidated financial statements and notes thereto, included in Item 8 of this Report.

SELECTED FINANCIAL DATA

(dollars in millions, except per share data)

As of and for the year ended	Sept. 2, 2018 (52 weeks)	Sept. 3, 2017 (53 weeks)	Aug. 28, 2016 (52 weeks)	Aug. 30, 2015 (52 weeks)	Aug. 31, 2014 (52 weeks)
RESULTS OF OPERATIONS					
Net sales	$ 138,434	$ 126,172	$116,073	$113,666	$110,212
Membership fees	3,142	2,853	2,646	2,533	2,428
Gross margin[1] as a percentage of net sales	11.04%	11.33%	11.35 %	11.09 %	10.66%
Selling, general and administrative expenses as a percentage of net sales	10.02%	10.26%	10.40 %	10.07 %	9.89%
Operating income	$ 4,480	$ 4,111	$ 3,672	$ 3,624	$ 3,220
Net income attributable to Costco	3,134	2,679	2,350	2,377	2,058

If you look under Net Income attributable to Costco you'll see the figure $3,134 in millions, so Costco had a profit of $3.13 billion in 2018.

Let's say you were thinking of investing in NVIDIA. Just do a quick search for "NVIDIA Annual Report" and you'll find annual reports going back many years. For our purposes, let's look at the 2018 Annual Report.

Here's the cover of NVIDIA's most recent annual report:

Flip to the for "Selected Financial Data" to find this:

ITEM 6. SELECTED FINANCIAL DATA

The following selected financial data should be read in conjunction with our financial statements and the notes thereto, and with Item 7, "Management's Discussion and Analysis of Financial Condition and Results of Operations." The Consolidated Statements of Income data for fiscal years 2019, 2018, and 2017 and the Consolidated Balance Sheets data as of January 27, 2019 and January 28, 2018 have been derived from and should be read in conjunction with our audited consolidated financial statements and the notes thereto included in Part IV, Item 15 in this Annual Report on Form 10-K. We operate on a 52- or 53-week year, ending on the last Sunday in January. Fiscal years 2019, 2018, 2017, and 2015 were 52-week years and fiscal year 2016 was a 53-week year.

	Year Ended				
	January 27, 2019	January 28, 2018	January 29, 2017	January 31, 2016 (A)	January 25, 2015
Consolidated Statements of Income Data:	(In millions, except per share data)				
Revenue	$ 11,716	$ 9,714	$ 6,910	$ 5,010	$ 4,682
Income from operations	$ 3,804	$ 3,210	$ 1,934	$ 747	$ 759
Net income	$ 4,141	$ 3,047	$ 1,666	$ 614	$ 631
Net income per share:					
Basic	$ 6.81	$ 5.09	$ 3.08	$ 1.13	$ 1.14
Diluted	$ 6.63	$ 4.82	$ 2.57	$ 1.08	$ 1.12
Weighted average shares used in per share computation:					
Basic	608	599	541	543	552
Diluted	625	632	649	569	563

We have already discussed Zoom Video Communications, so here you can see a screenshot from Zoom's Form S-1 that shows the company was profitable in the year ended 1/31/2019.

	Year Ended January 31,		
	2017	2018	2019
	(in thousands, except share and per share data)		
Consolidated Statements of Operations Data:			
Revenue	$ 60,817	$ 151,478	$ 330,517
Cost of revenue[1]	12,472	30,780	61,001
Gross profit	48,345	120,698	269,516
Operating expenses:			
Research and development[1]	9,218	15,733	33,014
Sales and marketing[1]	31,580	82,707	185,821
General and administrative[1]	7,547	27,091	44,514
Total operating expenses	48,345	125,531	263,349
Income (loss) from operations	—	(4,833)	6,167

The software company Twilio is not making a profit: here you can see from the net loss that they company is losing money.

	Year Ended December 31,				
	2018	2017	2016	2015	2014
	(In thousands, except share, per share and customer data)				
Consolidated Statement of Operations Data:					
Revenue	$ 650,067	$ 399,020	$ 277,335	$ 166,919	$ 88,846
Cost of revenue[1][2]	300,841	182,895	120,520	74,454	41,423
Gross profit	349,226	216,125	156,815	92,465	47,423
Operating expenses:					
Research and development[1][2]	171,358	120,739	77,926	42,559	21,824
Sales and marketing[1][2]	175,555	100,669	65,267	49,308	33,322
General and administrative[1][2]	110,427	59,619	51,077	35,991	18,960
Charitable contribution	7,121	1,172	3,860	—	—
Total operating expenses	464,461	282,199	198,130	127,858	74,106
Loss from operations	(115,235)	(66,074)	(41,315)	(35,393)	(26,683)
Other income (expenses), net	(5,923)	3,071	317	11	(62)
Loss before provision for income taxes	(121,158)	(63,003)	(40,998)	(35,382)	(26,745)
Provision for income taxes	(791)	(705)	(326)	(122)	(13)
Net loss	(121,949)	(63,708)	(41,324)	(35,504)	(26,758)

The software company mongoDB is not making a profit: here you can see from the net loss that they company is losing money.

	Years Ended January 31,			
	2019	2018 *As Adjusted	2017 *As Adjusted	2016*
	(in thousands, except share and per share data)			
Consolidated Statements of Operations Data:				
Revenue:				
Subscription	$ 248,391	$ 151,853	$ 104,033	$ 58,561
Services	18,625	14,175	10,772	6,710
Total revenue	267,016	166,028	114,805	65,271
Cost of revenue:				
Subscription[1]	56,255	30,766	19,352	13,146
Services[1]	17,313	12,093	10,515	7,715
Total cost of revenue	73,568	42,859	29,867	20,861
Gross profit	193,448	123,169	84,938	44,410
Operating expenses:				
Sales and marketing[1]	148,296	109,073	75,413	56,613
Research and development[1]	89,854	62,202	51,772	43,465
General and administrative[1]	53,063	36,775	27,082	17,070
Total operating expenses	291,213	208,050	154,267	117,148
Loss from operations	(97,765)	(84,881)	(69,329)	(72,738)
Other income (expense), net	(4,564)	2,195	(15)	(306)
Loss before provision for (benefit from) income taxes	(102,329)	(82,686)	(69,344)	(73,044)
Provision for (benefit from) income taxes	(3,318)	1,287	719	442
Net loss	$ (99,011)	$ (83,973)	$ (70,063)	$ (73,486)

Just see if that line that says "Net income" or "Net loss" and you'll instantly see if the company is profitable or not. If the profit number has parenthesis around it then the company is operating at a loss.

Comparing three cloud software companies

It makes sense to compare Zoom to other cloud-based software companies to compare apples to apples and get a reasonable idea of the stock price by comparing companies in the same industry (cloud-based software).

Let's compare the revenues (sales) for the most recent year to the market capitalization of the stock. Info about these companies and their sales numbers are easy to find with a quick search.

Zoom is a cloud-based video communications software program that lets people in different locations have video conferences using phones, tablets, computers, or Zoom rooms.

Twilio offers a cloud platform that enables developers to build, scale, and operate real-time communication within software applications. Examples include notifying a restaurant diner that their table is ready or a traveler when their flight is delayed.

MongoDB is a modern, cloud-based database platform. The platform enables developers to build and modernize applications rapidly and cost-effectively across a broad range of use cases.

We can compare the relationship between these companies' total revenues and market cap. Keep in mind that these are metrics used to compare revenue to market price, but *not intended to determine relative value* of one company to another.

Market Capitalizations

1. Zoom market cap $18.0 billion
2. Twilio market cap $14.5 billion
3. mongoDB market cap $6.6 billion

Revenues for most recent year

1. Zoom Revenues[1]: $330 million
2. Twilio Revenues[2] $650 million
3. mongoDB Revenues[3]: $267 million

If we divide market cap by revenues we get:

1. Zoom: $24.0 billion ÷ $330 million = 72.7
2. Twilio: $14.5 billion ÷ $650 million = 22.3
3. mongoDB: $6.6 billion ÷ $267 million = 24.7

Zoom is selling for about 73x revenue, Twilio for 22x revenue, and mongoDB for 25x revenue.

Keep in mind is that these numbers will change when the stock price changes (it affects the market cap) and when company revenues change. So the information above is a "snapshot" of a moment in time, and it changes daily.

I think it's useful to potential investors to try and figure out why these market gives these three companies vastly different multiples of price to revenues. More important, I think, is to ask the question: *Is Zoom expensive compared to the other two, or are the other two cheap compared to Zoom?*

Let's try to answer this based on what we know. First, as we saw in the earlier screenshots of the financial statements, Zoom is already profitable, and the other two are not. So investors are giving a higher multiple (in effect "paying a lot") for the stock of the company that's already profitable. Are they paying too much? That's anyone's guess. My guess is yes, but I could be wrong.

Also, Twilio and MongoDb are selling at multiples higher than 22x revenues, which I think is already expensive. So it could be that all cloud-computing stocks are overpriced right now.

Going back to determining a value for Zoom's stock price (I'm less interested in the other two companies, and only use them for comparison purposes) I would prefer to buy stock when the stock is selling in a range between 15x and 20x revenues.

$330 million (revenues) x 15 = $5.0 billion market cap
$330 million (revenues) x 20 = $6.6 billion market cap
Zoom's current valuation: $18 billion

The current valuation of $18 billion is about 4 times higher than the higher end of the multiple I'd be willing to pay, which values the whole company at $6.6 billion.

In other words, let's divide market cap by 292 million shares outstanding:

At the current $24 billion valuation the price per share is: $24,000,000,000 ÷ 292,000,000 = about $82/share.

At the $5.0 billion valuation (15x revenues) the price per share would be:

$5,000,000,000 \div 292,000,000 = about \, \$17/share$

At the \$6.6 billion valuation (20x revenues) the price per share would be:

$6,600,000,000 \div 292,000,000 = about \, \$23/share$

Looking at the current stock price it seems Zoom would have to decline in price by about 72.5% to get to a multiple of 20x revenues.

Will it ever get there? It's anyone's guess. My guess is that there are some "moving parts" going on right now in the background: Zoom's revenues are likely increasing, which would make the price we are willing to pay for each share of stock higher. Of course we don't know the exact numbers, so we can only guess.

I like Peter Lynch's reminder that you don't have to own every stock just because it has a cool product and its stock price has been going up steadily.

You don't have to "kiss all the girls." I've missed my share of ten baggers and it hasn't kept me from beating the market.

PETER LYNCH

I'm not buying this stock until the valuation changes, and that will definitely require the stock to decline in value from the \$80 price range, the company's profits to increase, or both. I have no control over the company and how it grows, but I do have control over the price I'll pay for the stock, and for now I'm not a buyer.

You will be better off investing only in profitable companies. It's true that there are many exciting unprofitable companies to think about, but I want to help you pass over the "not yet profitable" ones and invest in companies that are already successful. I want your investments to compound over time. I do not want you to have to wait for struggling companies to turn themselves around (unlikely to happen) or upstart companies to prove they can eventually turn a profit; those are both speculative ventures. I want to steer you away from speculation and toward investment.

Yes, it's exciting to be an early investor in a stock that everyone is talking about. You could own Tesla, Snapchat, Uber, Dropbox, Beyond Meat, Peloton, or any other hot stock that everyone is buying at insanely high prices. The problem with these "hot stocks" is that for every company that succeeds, several fail. It is difficult to know which ones will be spectacular successes and which will not. If you buy a hot stock there is a good chance you will have a breathtaking loss in stock price, and the loss may be so great you may never break even. The number one rule in investing is "don't lose money."

With investing, the good news is that you don't have to hit the ball over the fence every time. You just have to pick companies that are already profitable, already growing and you get to profit along with them for many years. There are fewer sleepless nights, less stress, and less hoping that your luck will change. That's all part of the gambling or speculating mindset. That is why I encourage you to skip over the not-yet-profitable companies and invest in those that are already a success.

Stick with big, easy decisions

Buffett made a bet that the S&P 500 index would be beat the performance of the best and brightest hedge fund managers over a 10 year period. He won by a landslide, and said the final lesson from the bet is to "Stick with big, 'easy' decisions and eschew activity."

Here's how Buffett explained the bet.

During the 10-year-bet, the 200-plus hedge-fund managers that were involved almost certainly made tens of thousands of buy and sell decisions. Most of those managers undoubtedly thought hard about their decisions, each of which they believed would prove advantageous. In the process of investing, they studied 10-Ks, interviewed managements, read trade journals and conferred with Wall Street analysts.

WARREN BUFFETT

Financial documents are written in the language of accounting. If you are not familiar with accounting, do not worry, you're going to be fine just learning the basics in this book. Because businesses describe their profitability and financial health in their annual reports, you will be better off if you understand these reports. You will be at a huge disadvantage if you can't read them.

However, keep in mind that all of the research, thinking, and analysis of financial statements is not enough to make you a great investor. If it were all you would have to do is spend a lot of time reading and you'd be rich. As the hedge-fund managers who proved when they wound up on the losing side of the bet against Buffett, analysis, brains and reading do not make a great investor. There are other traits like rationality, having a good temperament, and patience coupled with decisiveness, that are much more important; but I'm getting ahead of myself.

I want you to know that reading financials is not everything in investing; it's merely one component. If reading financial statements were crucial to picking to winning investments all hedge-fund managers would just devote time to reading. In Chapter 13 I'll show you how to read annual reports so you can find out the most important numbers in the annual report including whether the company is profitable.

SEVEN

A - ADAPTABLE

AS YOU CONSIDER any stock for investing, ask yourself "Is this company adapting quickly to new technology?" You want to focus on leading edge brands, and companies reaching their customers through mobile apps, great websites, using video intelligently and developing a strong social media presence.

Check out the company's website, its Apple Store or Google Play app, and see if customers give it high marks. You want to get a pulse of which companies are really "getting it" and evolving with the times to serve customers well. Starbucks uses a loyalty program to hook customers, and Nike has a series of segmented websites for sneakers, clothing, and definitely connects with customers using technology, including having a strong Instagram presence.

Other companies dropped the ball in using tech to relate to customers. L Brands, which owns Victoria's Secret, is an example of a company that fumbled big time — the company could have used digital media to connect with its client base — especially its younger customers through it's PINK brand. Instead, the company lost touch with its customers to American Eagle Outfitters' Aerie brand and other competitors. If a company you're thinking of buying seems even slightly out-of-step with customers, and is not using apps, social media and tech to form a strong bond to customers, look out!

It's much better to find companies that rapidly adapt to new technologies and provide services and products that attract customers.

Companies in today's business climate need to adapt quickly to changing technologies or they will perish. It doesn't matter what industry the company is in, they all need to change to meet consumer demands, and not be buried by the competition.

Here are a few examples of companies that adapt to new technologies. There are hundreds of other companies handling the task well, and I'm just mentioning a few familiar ones to give you an idea of the qualities of companies that adapt well to new technologies and anticipate customer wants and needs

Amazon

Amazon is constantly adapting to customers, and its CEO Jeff Bezos is devoted to constantly improving the customer experience. He believes that it's not the customer's job to tell you what they want, it's your job to constantly try to invent new products on behalf of customers.

A culture of innovation drives everything that Amazon does, and it's crucial to the "Always Day 1" mantra that Bezos claims is one of the keys to Amazon's success. The company retains the energy and drive to innovate and start-up mentality by always thinking as though the company needs to invent and adapt to customer desires and needs. He said that the goal is for Amazon to never become a "Day 2" company, where people get used to doing things the way they've always been done, when people get comfortable or complacent.

One of the keys to Amazon's success is that the company is always thinking of how to make its products cheaper and deliver them faster. With respect to faster delivery, Bezos says that now, and 10 years from now people will always want faster delivery. "A customer will never be unhappy because you delivered their order faster than expected," Bezos said. Adapting to consumer needs, and creating new technologies like Amazon's Echo are just a few of the many ways that Amazon constantly adapts new technologies to deliver the goods faster and cheaper than its competition.

Square

Square lets accept credit cards for retail transactions quickly and easily, and it also offers card swiping technology that lets small businesses accept credit cards and send invoices using smartphones. The company has adapted well to changes in retailing, and this bodes well for its future. For example, when credit cards changed to chip technology from swipe technology, Square quickly adapted and made chip-reading card readers available. When Starbucks needed a point-of-sale payment system in all of its stores, Square provided the system.

By continually innovating to become a useful feature of the retail landscape, Square ensures that it will not easily become irrelevant. The company has even made it possible for small businesses to create invoices on their mobile phone and send them to clients who can then pay the invoice with a credit card. This small innovation makes it very easy for the small business to get paid quickly and easily, and it ensures a secure transaction for the buyer as well.

Square's business adapts rapidly to changes in technology. They have consistently improved their apps and website offerings to anticipate the needs of small businesses and improve the retail experience.

Starbucks

Starbucks has adapted to the changing digital world by developing an app that is becoming heavily used by its customers. The Starbucks app lets customers pay for coffee, food, or other store products using the app, and when they purchase they earn "stars" which are part of a loyalty program that rewards regular users with drinks or food when they reach a certain number of stars earned.

The company has recognized rapid adoption of the app, with more users signing up every year since the app has been in use. Customers can order using the mobile app before they arrive in a cafe, and pick up their order once they arrive. Mobile ordering has not been without its problems, as some stores have had problems keeping up with the rapid adoption and in-store customers have had to wait as mobile orders are filled, but these bottlenecks have been addressed and with time will likely be fixed.

Companies that integrate technology and make it easy for customers to use their mobile devices will likely do well in the future, while those that are slow to adapt are surely going to be outcompeted by more nimble rivals.

EIGHT

L - LOYAL CUSTOMERS

LOYAL CUSTOMERS DRIVE SUCCESSFUL BRANDS. Loyalty is one of those qualities that can't easily be measured with math. A financial analyst can crunch numbers all they want, but you actually have an edge over Wall Street finance types in your ability to see early on which products have loyal fans.

Understanding customer loyalty toward a product or service is an enormous advantage to an investor, and you will benefit if you can use your first-hand knowledge of customer loyalty as your investing edge.

When you go to a favorite store and it's always packed with customers, you witness loyal behavior that Wall Street analysts might not see. When you notice that your friends all tend to buy the same kind of phone, or all like to go to the same restaurants, you have an edge. You probably know more than you think in this area.

Let me tell you about a few of my investing regrets: these are things that I knew enough to make an easy decision on several years ago, but for some reason I just thought I didn't know enough to buy the stock. Yet I was already a loyal user, and so were my friends and family, and that should have steered me toward a few great stocks.

1. Google went public in 2004 and I never even thought of buying the stock. I was a more cautious investor then and I was kind of scared to invest in tech because one the investors I admired, Warren Buffett, was also tech-averse. So while I was comfortable owning shares of Berkshire Hathaway (I bought them a year before the Google IPO) I never bought Google. But here's the problem: Google was the only search engine I used, and it's the only one all of my friends used too. It had the most loyal following of all search engines, and I never bought the stock! That's just plain stupid, looking back, and it's a lesson to me, and also to readers. If you and everyone you know are addicted to a service or product, then it's likely other people are too. You want to seriously consider those stocks.

2. Facebook went public in 2012, and I was never interested in that stock. I was one of those people who was last to set up an account for myself, and even with one I rarely ever posted. So I cut myself slack for that, because I didn't really know the company that well. But the game-changer was Instagram, and that was Facebook's best acquisition — possibly the best purchase of one company by another in the modern era. I used Instagram, and I could see others starting to use it a lot several years ago, and it never "clicked" in my mind that buying Facebook stock would make me a shareholder in the company that owns Instagram. So in the future, if I'm loyal to an app like Instagram — and most people who use it have serious habits — that's a good signal that the brand has serious loyalty.

3. Apple is one of those brands with incredible customer loyalty. I'm not saying it's the best mobile phone, and I know that other companies make fantastic devices, but I'm just talking loyalty. People who own iPhones usually

get another iPhone, and another. Also, people who have MacBook Pro laptops replace them with MacBook Pros. Apple customers buy iPads, iWatches, and iPods. The company has this huge loyal customer base, and they not only buy the hardware, they also buy apps, music, movies, and many other services that Apple offers. When it comes to customer loyalty, it doesn't get much better than Apple.

Wall Street analysts may be good when it comes to making complex calculations, but they don't have an edge over you when it comes to first-hand information that customers like you possess. Just think, every time you buy things online or visit stores you are learning about companies. You already know a lot about several companies just based on where you spend your money. Your unique retail experiences give you a huge advantage over financial analysts who lack the kind of direct experience you have with the brands you like.

The three companies listed above are three of the most successful companies of our time, and I'd say their loyal users have a lot to do with that. So your homework, as you search for the next great stock you're interested in buying, is to use the loyalty question to determine what brands are getting traction.

Look at your own patterns, and pay attention to people around you. Also, make sure you're looking at the behaviors of people younger than you, because — especially with new technology — they young crowd is usually on the leading edge when it comes to diving what is cool and what will soon be in demand. As they get older, they'll have the purchasing power to buy. So they are your guides to where strong loyalty is starting to develop right now.

Thinking about loyalty gives you an extra tool in your tool belt that not every investor uses, and when you combine it with other filters you're starting to use a "multi-pronged" approach to investing. There is a saying, "To a man with a hammer, every problem is a nail." Well, if all you use is math to evaluate companies, then you're at a huge disadvantage when you go up against someone with many more tools in their tool belt, and superhero power to see loyalty is powerful indeed.

I searched Google for "Brands With Most Loyal Customers" and found this list.[1] Brand Keys, the consultancy that conducted the survey, looked at 740 brands to arrive at these 20 companies:

1. Amazon (online retail)
2. Google
3. Apple (tablets)
4. Netflix
5. Apple (smartphones)
6. Amazon (video streaming)
7. Samsung
8. Facebook
9. Amazon (tablets)
10. YouTube
11. Dunkin' Donuts
12. Nike
13. Trader Joe's
14. WhatsApp
15. iTunes
16. Hyundai
17. Starbucks
18. Ford
19. PayPal
20. Domino's

These are powerful insights into these companies, and how customers relate to them. These brands have a place in customers' hearts. You can't learn of these "intangible" qualities by combing through financial statements, but if you are a customer of these (or other) companies, then you probably have some unique understanding about customer loyalty that another investor might not posses.

It makes sense to incorporate customer loyalty into a filtering system. It tells us that customers feel something "emotional" or a "bond" to the brand, and over time this can help a company fend off competition. You can call it stickiness or loyalty or whatever you'd like, but the important "take-home" message is that if you can identify companies with strong loyalty, you are likely to have found a company that will continue to have a stream of revenue from these clients for many years into the future. As you can see, from the list above, Amazon and Apple appear twice on the list for loyalty for different products.

There are many companies that have loyal followings. I will provide one example below that I know well because of all of my experience as a professional photographer. I use Adobe products (Photoshop and Lightroom) every day and I also know many photographers. I can say without hesitation that every serious photographer uses Photoshop.

I'll explain why Adobe exemplifies a business with loyal customers. I hope you'll take a moment to ask yourself how if a company that you're considering for investment has loyal customers. One way to define loyal customers is repeat buyers who will be unlikely to switch to a competitor because they have a personal connection with the brand, they feel an almost irrational connection to the products, and they use them reflexively. If the brand name is also a verb, that's a good sign that the company has loyal devotees: think Fedex, Photoshop, etc.

Adobe Systems

Adobe makes the best photo editing software system on earth. There are no serious competitors out there. I'm not saying there are not some image editing programs available, but none where the name of the program has become a verb like "Photoshopping."

Based as it is on familiarity going back more than 20 years, Adobe's products like Photoshop, Illustrator, InDesign, Lightroom, and Premiere Pro have formed a strong bond with photographers, designers, filmmakers and marketers alike. The loyalty is intense; I don't know of a single photographer who doesn't use Photoshop, nor do I know any designers who don't use Illustrator or InDesign regularly.

Adobe has millions of loyal customers for its products, and enjoys very little competition because of the "switching cost" of time that users of software like Photoshop, Illustrator and Premiere would be required to spend to learn how to use a competitor's products. This "learning hurdle" ensures that Adobe will retain loyal users for years to come.

GEICO

GEICO is a wholly-owned subsidiary of Berkshire Hathaway Corp., and while you can't buy stock in GEICO directly, it's a great example of a company that has loyal customers.[2] The company's overall cost structure is low, and by selling directly to the consumer they avoid having to pay rent for retail locations, etc. Their service is top notch, which means they retain customers, and this in turn makes for a solid business model because they have frequent renewals, which translates into less money spent trying to retain customers. They simply renew and this process makes keeping customers inexpensive.

Clearly, customer loyalty is an enormous part of GEICO's success. They have a large and growing customer base, and these customers spread the world, and gradually the company's market share has grown.

As you search for companies as investments, you would be well served by looking for companies like GEICO that have a low cost structure, have been growing their market share consistently over time, and have many loyal and happy customers.

Nike

Nike is one of the great all-time brands, and has a loyal following. There's not a lot to be said about the company that people in all countries don't already understand. They started with sneakers and branched out into all kinds of athletic apparel. They have remained relevant over the years to older generations while appealing to the young. I recently had the chance to make friends with people in my seat row on a recent flight from San Diego to Seattle, and one young man (high school age) told me he has a business of buying new Nike sneakers when they are released, and selling them (on eBay) at a huge markup to people who want those sneakers.

I'm not privy to all of the hype and excitement about the Nike brand, but the company has found a way to appeal to people and make shoes that are not only worn for sports and fashion, but collected as artwork. Nike undoubtedly knows about this attraction (they created the demand for it, after all) and they have found a way to release some sneakers in limited supply so as not to flood the market.

The constant innovation, finger on the pulse of fashion and sports, and awareness of the importance of scarcity all point to the intelligence of a company that straddles the worlds of art, athletics, and commerce. The way they connect with customers' hearts and minds as well as their bodies ensures that the Nike brand will remain relevant for many years to come. As an investor, you want to be on the lookout for companies with many loyal customers; they make repeat business and consistent cash flows more likely, and improve your odds of long-term investment success.

Loyal customers mean repeat business

Companies that have loyal customers don't have to keep spending money acquiring or retaining new customers, and that saves them tons of money. Recurring streams of income are the life blood of a company, and the companies that have loyal customers can basically print their own money — they have fresh sources of cash flowing in every day. If you have any question about that, take a look at Apple's cash position. They are not only one of the most profitable companies in the world, they get so much cash they just stockpile it.

Leadership

Even though this chapter is titled "L - Loyal" I just wanted to let you know that leadership is another insanely important "L" when it comes to picking stocks. Leaders with talent and integrity are a vital part of any company that you consider for investment. I have thought that the "L" in the PALMS filtering system could (and an argument could be made that it should) stand for "Leaders" instead of Loyalty.

To be clear, when I talk about leaders I'm talking about the CEO of a company, and in some cases, such as Berkshire Hathaway's, I'm talking about the partnership of Buffett and Munger who together have led the company for decades. Outstanding leadership is hard to define with numbers, but it can really make a company great. Think of Bezos' role at Amazon or Jobs at Apple and you can see how having a leader with a clear vision and ability to make a few great decisions each year can be of enormous benefit to a company. Take away that leader and the company floats aimlessly or sinks. Many great companies have been ruined by lousy leaders.

It is hard to tell you how to know what leaders are great and will continue to make intelligent decisions in the future, and which ones will flounder. These things are often apparent after the fact, but if you're not investing in a large company with a well-known CEO then it is very difficult to gauge the talent and integrity of someone you've never met.

For this reason I choose "Loyal" for the L because we all know about brands with loyal customers, and the brands like Nike, Google, Apple will probably be around in 10, 20, or 30 years (or more) and they will be earning a lot more money in the future than they are now. The leaders will come and go, and some will be good and some will not, and it's a very difficult task for any investor to try and assess the talent of a CEO before investing.

I would say that it makes sense to learn as much as you can about the CEO, to watch some YouTube videos, read articles, and of course read the company's annual report before you invest. If you agree with the CEO's letter and you believe they understand their industry, the company, and get as good an idea as possible if you think they are talented and capable enough to carry out their plan. This is an almost impossible task (to predict the unpredictable) yet that is why investing is so challenging. If you buy stock in a company that is run by people with high integrity and with loads of talent, everything else will fall into place.

So I stick to my advice of searching for companies with loyal customers who are likely to come back and buy again and again, yet I also want to encourage you to keep your eyes out for the other "L" and look for leaders with high ethical standards and the ability to make a few great decisions each year.

NINE

M - MOAT

AN INVESTING MOAT IS A BUSINESS' ability to resist competition and protect its long-term profits. A strong brand, unique product, or superior service create a moat around a business that makes it very difficult for competitors to break in and peel away some of the company's customers, just as a moat defends a castle against attacks.

You want to buy stock in a few outstanding businesses and not worry about their ability to earn profits for years to come. If you invest in businesses that have these "moats" you won't have to worry about your investment from year to year. You can just buy the stock, sit back, and kick your feet up.

The following drawing shows Bob, The King of Squirrels, flanked by bodyguards in ninja hoodies who protect the castle and its prized stash of acorns. A hungry alligator patrols the moat, ready to devour any creatures who try to swim across. The hungry squirrel and its beaver companions are trying to figure out how to cross the moat to get acorns.

A moat is a deep, wide ditch filled with water that surrounds a castle to defend itself against attacks from invaders. Moats around businesses are protective barriers that make it hard for competitors to duplicate a company's success and take away their market share. Strong brands, products, services, and cultures all contribute to the strength of moats, and great companies continually look for ways to widen them.

A wide range of companies like Nike, Apple, Coke, Disney, McDonald's, Home Depot, Costco, Google, Boeing, Microsoft, Starbucks, and Amazon all have wide moats that protect their businesses. Most companies either have no moat or a narrow moat, so a wide moat is a powerful attribute.

Starbuck's moat is the consistency of its cafe experience no matter what country you're in, the many locations of its stores across the world, and the growing power of the Starbucks brand and its recognizability across the world, from the USA to South America, Europe, Brazil and China.

Berkshire Hathaway owns many companies with moats, such as GEICO, which offers low cost car insurance. Car insurance is considered a commodity by many people, and GEICO's moat is being the lowest cost provider.

Amazon's moat is the company's customer obsession. It provides the selection, price, and fast delivery at a level that's never existed before. If you wanted to start your own online retailer and try to outcompete Amazon you probably couldn't do it. That's the effect of a wide moat.

Moats are dynamic

The moat surrounding a business is dynamic. Few businesses are content to have a static moat, and the best companies are continually widening their moat by providing new products or services, a cheaper product or service, or strengthening the customer bond. In this chapter we'll look at Coke, Pepsi, Microsoft, Apple and GEICO and see why each company has a moat. One important question I want you to ask when looking at a company is whether the moat is getting wider or narrower. All great businesses have leaders who find ways to widen the moat and protect their fortress.

To grasp why this is such an important distinction, you really want to buy stock once and forget about it.[1] Since you only want to have to make one buy decision and not have to look at the stock and wonder if you should sell it, you should aim to buy stock in a business that's widening the moat, and not one where the moat is shrinking.

As an example of how you need to dig a bit to find out if a moat is shrinking or widening, let's look Coca-Cola, McDonald's and Star-bucks. I've read and heard a lot in the media about about people making "healthier" choices which seem to suggest that consumers are drinking fewer soft drinks and eating fast food less often. Do these statements correspond to the data? I researched the stock price returns of Coca-Cola, McDonald's, and Starbucks over the past three-, five-, 10- and 15-year periods[2] compared to the S&P 500 index. Keep in mind these are relative results, meaning they show the extent to which each company's stock has outperformed the "aver-age" US company. Stock prices are not perfect indicators of business success, but when a company does well its stock price generally follows. Here are the stock price returns for these three companies:

1-year returns

- Coca-Cola: 19.00%
- McDonald's: 33.11%
- Starbucks: 62.17%

3-year returns

- Coca-Cola: 11.38%
- McDonald's: 23.96%
- Starbucks: 20.72%

5-year returns

- Coca-Cola: 7.79%
- McDonald's: 19.38%
- Starbucks: 20.14%

10-year returns

- Coca-Cola: 9.44%
- McDonald's: 15.58%
- Starbucks: 25.03%

It's worth noting is that Coca-Cola has had lagged the performance of Starbucks and McDonald's over all time periods shown above. To be fair, a more accurate comparison would be with Pepsi or another beverage company. I chose the comparison with McDonald's and Starbucks to show how both companies have been grown faster during the past decade. McDonald's has outperformed Coke, and Starbucks' has been growing at a rapid pace.

Coca-Cola's moat may be narrowing for a variety of reasons. Its relative performance was more robust in previous decades, but consumer tastes may be changing. It's difficult to know for sure, but Coke may be vulnerable if people start to choose "healthier" alternatives. Not only is Coke underperforming relative to McDonald's and Starbucks, it's losing to the S&P 500 as well.

It's hard to know what, exactly, accounts for Coke's underperformance relative to the S&P 500, but I would guess that their competition is cutting into their profits. More people may be drinking Juice, LaCroix water, Kombucha, Red Bull, Smoothies, or going to Starbucks. Whatever the reason, the market is not as excited about Coca-Cola over the last decade as it had been in the past.

McDonald's and Starbucks seem to be growing their businesses faster than Coca-Cola and also widening their moats. You can easily find the total stock returns for any company with a quick online search useful to see if a company's is performing well over long periods of time (especially 5- and 10-year periods) to see if the moat is widening or narrowing.

You want to stack things in your favor before you invest, and you can do this by searching for companies with moats that will protect them in the future like the moats around McDonald's and Starbucks. You don't need to own stock in many businesses like those to get rich.

Which companies will dominate?

The key to investing is *not to guess if an industry* will benefit society, or how fast it will grow, but *which company within the industry* will have a competitive advantage and how long that will last.

Let me share two examples:

1. *Electric cars* – I have no doubt that electric cars, or gas/electric hybrids will only increase in popularity. If I were to invest in this area I would want to be able to predict, with a high degree of certainty, which company would have an advantage over all the others. Tesla gets constant media attention for obvious reasons, and especially because Elon Musk has become a celebrity and Tweets regularly.

But is it possible that already established auto makers could dominate the electric or hybrid industry? It could be that Tesla could run out of money or somehow make critical mistakes that doom the business. I would say that it is difficult to know at this early juncture who will dominate the electric car industry. The existing car makers (BMW, GM, Ford, Porsche, Volkswagen, Honda and Toyota) already have profitable businesses.

You can assume that they have engineers taking apart Teslas and examining every detail of the hardware and software used, and trying to figure out how to improve upon the design. These car manufacturers already have plants, employees, and processes in place.

Again, this is nothing against Tesla or its leader, it's just an observation; there's no way to know with certainty if Tesla will have a competitive advantage in electric cars five or 10 years from now. They may be just one of many companies making electric cars, and they may have no moat, and be constantly struggling to keep up with competition. On the other hand, if they do have the "secret sauce" of electric vehicle creation and production, then they could become dominant electric car maker and widen their moat. It's still too early to know for sure.

2. *Mobile Phones* – Among my cohort the iPhone is the mobile device that most people aspire to own, and it was clearly the first mobile device to combine music, photos, video, Internet browsing and email in one package with an app store in one small package with excellent design. The question I would have about investing in Apple is this: is Apple's moat, which is wide due to customer loyalty, going to continue to grow, or are the company's best days in the past and its moat is shrinking?

I believe Apple will survive the flood of competition over the next several years because it has so many loyal users, and a stickiness to Apple products, and most loyal customers will not want to switch to another phone. The company is the most profitable smartphone maker on the planet[3] and they have stockpiled a lot of cash to fund research & development. Even if they don't innovate as they have in the past, it seems as though their current customers will buy again and again[4], and that gives the company a moat, though I don't think it's a wide moat. It seems narrow at the moment due to competition, and it's anyone's guess if Apple's moat is widening or shrinking.

Apple faces steep competition from Samsung and Huawei, whose phone sales have been growing faster than Apple or Samsung's[5]. It's anyone's guess how much worldwide competition Apple will face from these new phones, but there is a possibility that the competition could innovate more quickly and bring new technologies to their devices before Apple.

One aspect of Apple's current moat is that the company is a luxury brand, and many people who buy iPhones either consciously or unconsciously are signaling their good taste or financial status by paying top dollar for their phones. That is a huge plus for Apple, because it ensures loyalty from this segment of customers, and knowing that someone will likely buy future devices from you (iPads, MacBooks, iWatches, iPods, etc) is a huge wind at your back.

But the question for an investor is whether this moat is widening, or whether things are going to get more difficult for Apple in the future as the advantage that the company had with Steve Jobs and Jony Ive[6], the outgoing chief design officer of Apple, will disappear. The innovation and design of future iPhones are in the hands of new people, and it is uncertain whether the pace of invention will continue and Apple's moat will persist.

Competitors are not enemies

It's worth asking whether two companies seem like competitors can both have moats. At first glance, it looks like Apple and Microsoft are competitors. Does this mean that one of them has a moat and the other doesn't? It's a good question and worth digging a bit for the answer.

Both companies have competed with one another in the past (the hot debate of "Which is better, Mac or PC?" but that competition does not affect their moats in the competitive market. Sure, some people will prefer one operating system over the other for video games, writing, coding or doing Photoshop work, but those are specific niches for individual users and people tend to gravitate toward the system that works best for their specific needs.

If you look at the Latin root of "competition" you'll see it comes from the Latin roots "com-" meaning "with" and "petere" meaning "to seek." Put together they form the Latin word "competere," which means to strive together. Competitors can strive together without being enemies, and this seems to be the case with Apple and Microsoft which are both wide moat tech companies. One of them can grow and innovate without directly harming the other. There are some areas where companies compete directly – for example Microsoft for years has attempted to popularize a Windows phone, but without much success. If this device had taken off then Microsoft would be a strong competitor with Apple in the smartphone category. But that never happened and Apple is primarily a device company and Microsoft sells software.

Apple and Microsoft

Apple and Microsoft both have moats, but they're different moats. Apple's special bond is through selling devices and apps to retail customers, and Microsoft's bond is selling software to corporate customers. Each company can widen its moat without harming the other.

Apple is the dominant smartphone maker by making quality devices, and creating the iPhone, which has become such a powerful status symbol that communicates the success and desirability of its owner to others.

Microsoft dominates corporate America's operating system software. Other companies have tried to drink their milkshake (Linux, for example) but failed. I have not seen any software companies that pose a serious threat to Microsoft's dominance. Microsoft has also had massive success with their Azure cloud computing segment.

Apple and Microsoft compete in the field of computer hardware and software without being enemies. Each company has a moat, and each grows its own moat without destroying the other.

Apple can succeed by innovating and coming up with better iPhones without damaging Microsoft (except the possibility that Microsoft will have to scrap the Windows phone if nobody buys them!)[7]

Microsoft can succeed by improving Windows operating system, Word, Excel, Powerpoint, and improving its Azure cloud services.

The iPhone provides stickiness

Apple dominates Smartphone makers, as the iPhone is more than just a phone, it's a status symbol. It shows the world that you have money and are successful, and this widens a company's moat.

NYU professor Scott Galloway sees Apple as a luxury brand like Louis Vuitton, characterized by an iconic founder and "temples to the brand" (Apple Stores).[8]. He says that people use their iPhones to signal their desirability to others.

"Your No. 1 instinct is survival and, once that box is checked and you think, 'I'm going to make it through the day,' your No. 2 instinct is procreation," Galloway said.[9] "The No. 1 signal of wealth, the No. 1 signal of power, the No. 1 signal of your likelihood of a random sexual encounter in a greater selection set among potential mates is the iPhone."

Galloway says that and iPhone is a new signaling device. "An iPhone is saying to the opposite sex, or a potential mate, 'I have good genes. You should mate with me,'" Galloway said.

Apple's moat may be widening as they gain more loyal customers. It seems as though iPhone users do not want a low-priced phone to replace their iPhone when the time comes for a new one. That is Apple's moat; virtually all iPhone users replace their existing iPhones with another iPhone. There are not a lot of retail products like that, where loyalty is almost guaranteed. There are iPads and MacBooks and Apple watches, but those are extra products that round out Apple's world, but the company basically lives and dies by the iPhone now.

Whether this loyalty to Apple products will continue indefinitely is anyone's guess. I believe that going forward, Apple's success will depend mostly on the iPhone and not the iPods, iPad, iWatch, AirPods or MacBooks. The company is well-capitalized and not likely to disappear anytime soon, but whether they will continue to widen their moat by improving their iPhones and keeping customers loyal reminds to be seen. Some articles suggest that some iPhone users are dumping iPhones and buying Samsung. I have not seen this happen, but it doesn't mean it's not so. I think a potential investor in Apple should take a close look at whether the company's dominance seems assured for the next decade, and ask if the businesses' moat is widening or narrowing[10].

Some say the iPhone isn't necessarily the best smartphone. The best Android phones, some could argue, are out-designing the iPhone. Devices like Samsung's Galaxy S8 have features that just aren't available on Apple's flagship phones. Yet Apple is far in front and owns the lion's share of the smartphone industry's profits: iPhone owners are far more loyal than any Android owners.[11] According to a recent Morgan Stanley survey by Statista, 92% of iPhone owners who plan to get a new phone in the next 12 months say they're "somewhat or extremely likely" to stick with Apple. That trend, if it continues into the future, bodes well for Apple's moat.

The iPhone is an iconic device. Customers from China, Australia, Africa, Brazil and Israel may speak different languages, but they all share a common tool of communication, the iPhone, and they will go to great lengths to get one. As evidenced by the long lines outside Apple Stores in the United States, the demand is powerful. People in other countries go great lengths to get iPhones, and pay much higher prices in their currencies. The iPhone is a luxury device, a status symbol, an Internet device, a music player, and a personal computer — all in a package that fits in the pocket.

The Apple App Store continues to widen Apple's moat by making it easier for developers to make money by creating apps which are useful to iPhone users. The ease and ubiquity of Apps make them like tiny little drug deals dishing out dopamine hits to the masses. Some people have only 5 apps on their phone, while some have 50 or 500. These apps are continually updated, with new ones released every day, and combined they make up an ecosystem that's unmatched in the smartphone world.

Microsoft: emerging from stagnancy

Microsoft is not nearly as sleek or sexy as Apple, but they appeal more to corporate customers and less to retail customers. Instead of beautifully designed devices, Microsoft creates the Windows operating system for business and now the Azure cloud computing segment. Their products are in demand in the work place. Microsoft offers consistency and reliability to business customers around the world.

Microsoft had a period of stagnancy where people disliked its software, phones, and everything it touched. The company has its fingers in many pies, trying to (unsuccessfully) sell a Windows phone and also a personal assistant, Cortana, in what looks like a hail-Mary attempt to keep up with Apple's Siri.

With former CEO Steve Ballmer out of the picture, Microsoft is finding new success under CEO Satya Nadella who has reinvigorated Microsoft with Azure, the company's cloud services segment.

Azure has been a game-changer for Microsoft, and Azure now makes up 30% of Microsoft's revenues. In a few short years Microsoft under Nadella became a fast-growing cloud services company, and they did so blowing by Google to make it a two horse race with Amazon Web Services (AWS) which is still the #1 force in cloud computing. The Windows operating system remains Microsoft's cash cow, but Azure is quickly becoming Microsoft's other source of strength and further widens Microsoft's dominance in the corporate software market.

Coke & Pepsi's moats

Two competing companies like Coca-Cola and Pepsi can each have moats. Coke has more loyal customers, better beverage market share, higher profit margins, and greater presence in restaurants and stores around the world.[12] Coke is leader worldwide when it comes to soft drinks.

The ubiquity of the Coca-Cola brand make it one of the most recognizable brands on the planet, and are the basis for the company's wide moat. You could buy stock in Coke and just forget about it, and know that the company will be around 10 or 20 years from now

— just as it has since 1892. There is no sure way of knowing if the moat is widening or shrinking, but it does exist.

Pepsi's also has a wide moat, but it's mainly attributable to the company's food business. Snacks like Doritos, Lays Potato Chips and Quaker Oats drive about half of Pepsi's revenue and contribute more profit to the bottom line than Pepsi's beverage arm, mainly because of Frito-Lay's market dominance — because Frito-Lay has about 25% of the global market share of the potato chip market, compared to single-digit share for competitors.

So while Coca-Cola is the first name in soft drinks, Pepsi is most profitable selling chips in grocery stores and convenience stores and at gas stations, and that enhances the brand and gives Pepsi its wide moat.

GEICO's moat

GEICO sells car insurance, something that most customers view as a commodity. Everyone needs car insurance, and it's hard to tell the difference between insurers. You already know that GEICO's moat is that it offers the cheapest insurance, they remind you in every ad that if you call their toll-free number you'll probably find that you can save 15% on car insurance.[13]

When you start looking at companies you're considering as stock investments, keep your eyes open to the different qualities that make a moat. Amazon is so devoted to customers that it's often the first place they look when they need a great price and want something delivered fast. Apple makes beautifully designed technology that tells other people you've got taste.

GEICO is the lowest-cost insurance. Look for companies that are so good at what they do that you know you can just buy the stock and not have to look at it for 10 or 20 years because the company is so good at what it does, and has such loyal customers that they will succeed without you having to check up on them every day, week, month or week. Companies with moats make your decision easy, and they deliver one present surprise after another instead of one problem after another.

The Darwinian struggle

Businesses usually begin small, often selling one product or service, and with time they either grow to dominate their niche and become a fringe player, or they fade into obscurity. If you can find the businesses that will dominate their industry for years to come you'll be at an enormous advantage.

Competition is tough; each company engages in a vicious Darwinian struggle for survival. Every company tries to produce a product or a service that will attract customers and their dollars. And every business strives to come up with better products for their customers to buy. Even the best companies cannot afford to become complacent; they have to stay one step ahead of the competition always nipping at their heels, always trying to make better and cheaper products and deliver them faster.

Just look at the iPhone. It's one of the most popular smartphones in the world[14], and as anyone who owns one, or has family or friends who own one, it's a sticky product. What I mean by that is that when an iPhone user is ready to buy a new smartphone in a few years, there's a high likelihood that they'll buy another iPhone.

That kind of brand loyalty gives Apple a moat. It means if they can get a large number of people into their ecosystem and buying their iPhones (and chargers, cables, and other dongles), then they can continue selling them more devices in the future. If you imagine the company being a castle, the tendency of customers to stay loyal to Apple provides the moat.

Competitors nipping at your heels

Even terrific companies like Apple have to put forth a lot of effort in staying ahead of the curve. As successful as the iPhone has been, there is no guarantee that it will be the dominant phone 10 or 20 years from now. Steve Jobs set a high bar for innovation, but it's unclear if his successors will be able to continue to innovate at the rapid pace that it did under its founder.

As you read this, companies like Google, Huawei and Samsung are making great strides to take away iPhone market share. In fact, the Samsung Galaxy Note 10+ , the Samsung Galaxy S10 Plus are all giving the iPhone XS Max steep competition. The wide moat that Apple enjoys with its iPhone could start to narrow quickly if the company slips up, or even fails to innovate as quickly as its competitors.

Amazon made an attempt to break into the smartphone market with the Fire Phone, and though that was not a success, one cannot count Amazon out of the smartphone game just yet.

While Apple has a moat around their business (their iPhone franchise) there is no way to know for sure that this moat will endure a heavy siege. It seems safe for now, but the corporate highway is strewn with the roadkill of companies that didn't keep up with the competition.

Companies with moats dominate

Another way to think of a moat is a durable competitive advantage. It is what makes your company the top dog. Every sector of the economy usually has a company with a wide moat; the food and beverage industry has Coca-Cola, McDonald's, and Starbucks.

If a company lacks a moat then it's likely to suffer huge injuries when new companies burst through the castle walls. Earnings can fall short, new competitors will steal your customers, and your stock will crash 25% in a day because the business was not resistant to competition. Leo Tolstoy's Anna Karenina begins: "All happy families are alike; each unhappy family is unhappy in its own way."

The same would be said of happy businesses; they enjoy pleasant earnings surprises, grow businesses and widen moats. Each unhappy business is unhappy in its own way, losing money and customers while earnings erode because they are vulnerable to competition without a wide moat.

Finding moats

My goal is to teach you how to find moats on your own. You can, of course, take the shortcut and do a Google search for "companies with moats" but there are a few problems with that.

1. The moat you read about is not really that wide or it never existed.
2. The moat once existed but is now gone.
3. The articles you find may be poorly written, inaccurate, or biased. You can find better facts yourself.

But if you use caution and remain critical, it can't hurt to try a Google search for companies with moats; you may uncover some useful information.

Reading annual reports, watching videos where the CEO or other leaders are talking about their business will help you learn as much as you can about a company. You want to get a feel for whether a company is dominating its niche. Sometime you might hear a competitor refer to them as the ones to beat. Or maybe you'll notice that when they release a new product, everyone wants to buy them.

For example, I keep noticing people who seem to have good style sense wearing Nike sneakers. Now I have known the brand since I was a kid, and I still buy shirts or hats or sneakers from time to time, but I was not aware of how cutting edge the brand is today. There is a whole world of fashion, design, and an app called SNKRS[15], which Nike has been refining to connect super fans with desirable pairs of sneakers.[16]

I assure you that I'm not part of the fashion elite, but I do take note that Nike is not playing it safe and just making sneakers for sports. They spend a lot on advertising, and they push their sneakers and clothing into the spotlight as high fashion. I know it's working because on a recent flight the guy sitting next to me sporting bright white Nike high tops told me that he buys newly released rare Nike sneakers and then sells them on eBay for hundreds of dollars more than he paid.[17] It's his side hustle while going to school, and it seemed to be working for him. The fact that a huge company like Nike has created such demand for its products and kept them from being perceived as a cheap product or a commodity suggests it has a strong moat. Adidas, Under Armour, and Puma have many followers, but not the moat that Nike possesses.

Nike's North American position is about as dominant as they come. In 2016, it held 50.8 per cent of the U.S. retail brand footwear market, while Adidas improved its share to 7.4 per cent.[18]

The more you can read, watch videos, and learn about a company the better off you'll be forming an expert opinion about whether a moat exists.

To help you find companies with wide moats, I'll share with you a brief list of companies that I believe have wide moats.

All companies loosely fall into three categories: those that don't possess a moat, those with narrow moats, and those with wide moats. To keep things simple, I'm only interested in the latter.

Companies with moats I understand:[19]
   Adobe
   Alphabet
   Amazon
   Apple
   Berkshire Hathaway
   Costco
   Disney
   Intuitive Surgical
   McDonald's
   Microsoft

Nike
Starbucks
Waters

I believe all of these companies are, to some extent, resistant to competition and will continue to widen their moats.

I'll briefly describe Adobe and Intuitive Surgical, two wide-moat businesses that I don't own as of this writing.

Adobe

I'm familiar with Adobe through my experience as a photographer. The company develops Photoshop, a powerful photo-editing software program. Adobe also develops other software programs that photographers, graphic designers, and illustrators use: Lightroom, Illustrator, InDesign. In addition, Adobe's Premiere Pro is a powerful video editing program. All of Adobe's products are considered best-in-class and amount the most powerful tools used by visual professionals worldwide.

Because Adobe is usually the first choice of image-editing software used by creative professionals, Adobe essentially has a monopoly in creative software. There are many second and third-tier software options available, but none of them pose a serious threat to Adobe's dominance. One of the main reasons why Adobe's market wide moat is so secure is due to the high switching cost.

Any photographer, graphic designer, animator, illustrator, or filmmaker who wants to switch to other software and solution has to relearn a new interface. It can take several years to learn how to use new software, especially if that new software is difficult to master. Alternative software options may offer features that don't even stack up compared to Adobe's or it may not be compatible with their operating system. With so many unknown variables providing high switching costs, most professionals will likely stick to software they already understand. This stickiness provides Adobe with a wide moat to protect their customers from any competitor's offers.

Adobe provides terrific tools to artists, photographers, designers, marketing professionals, and filmmakers and they offer them as subscriptions, which encourages recurring monthly streams of income.

The wide range of people who use these products, the reality that few other products barely come close to competing, and the ease of use of the cloud-based subscription model all combine to provide a wide moat. Any new product innovations, such as Adobe's new foray into stock photography with Adobe Stock will only serve to widen the company's moat.

Intuitive Surgical

I first learned about this company many years ago. I was photographing heart surgery at the time, and one of the surgeons I worked with mentioned the "da Vinci" robotic-assisted surgical system developed by Intuitive Surgical (ISRG). This company has a moat because it has a large base of installed robotic machines.

As of March 31, 2018, Intuitive Surgical had 4,528 da Vinci surgical systems installed in hospitals and universities around the world. If you added all of its competitors together it would not even come close to Intuitive Surgical's installed base of robotic operating machines.

Intuitive Surgical has also spent several years training surgical staff on how to operate its machines, which range in price from $0.5 million to $2.5 million. This familiarity within the medical community is valuable because its users are unlikely to search beyond the da Vinci system for a long time to come. A competitor would have to start from scratch in developing not only the machines, but earning trust in the healthcare industry, which is tightly regulated and very resistant to change. In addition, the surgical staff who are already familiar with the da Vinci machines would have to learn how to use a totally new system. This learning curve provides a barrier to entry for any newcomer, which further widens Intuitive Surgical's moat.

The company also has excellent operating margins. The company not only makes money selling its expensive operating machines. In reality, these high-tech machines cost a lot to build, and when they're sold they yield low profit margins. Most of Intuitive Surgical's margins come from selling the instruments used with each procedure, and also from fixing the machines when they need service. The instrument and service categories will likely grow over time.

Because they are the only major robotic-assisted surgery machines in the world, and they help doctors do procedures with low risk of complication, Intuitive Surgical is a wide-moat business.

Intuitive Surgical is already used frequently in urology and gyne-cology surgeries, and it has lots of room to grow in colorectal, cardio-vascular, and general soft tissue surgical procedures. This lollapalooza of surgeries that its systems can address in a world that embraces technology as a way to save money and reduce surgical errors will provide a long runway and resistance from competition for years to come.

Some moats are hard to identify

I like the CVS pharmacy chain. I first saw them in my hometown of Newton, Massachusetts and have watched as they expanded across the country. I think they would probably be a good company to own, but I don't think they have a wide moat. I know they have competition from Walgreens, Costco, and Rite Aid and I imagine it's hard to have a wide moat in a commodity-type business of selling medications and retail pharmacy items.

It's too hard to know if CVS has a moat, so I just pass on making any decision about that stock. I simply don't know enough about the business, and if it will continue to be the dominant player in the phar-macy sector. Here is one main reason I'd be afraid of owning CVS for the long term: Amazon purchased PillPack Inc, a full service online pharmacy[20]. Its offer is that it helps users skip the pharmacy lines because the company sorts and delivers medication right to your door. If Amazon bought PillPack then it's definitely thinking of entering the online pharmacy business. If they did then stores like CVS and Walgreens would be much less valuable as their store traffic would drop. Much of a pharmacy's profit comes from snacks and other retail items sold to customers who visit a pharmacy to pick up prescriptions. If Amazon enters that market segment I would consider a large investment in a drugstore a precarious one at best.

How do you find moats?

What's the best way to find moats? Well, I'd hate to burst your bubble, but there is no shortcut. You have to learn about the company and do your homework. With time and reading you will start to figure out if a company had a moat or if it's just one of many companies fighting for scraps in an extremely competitive arena.

One thing I should mention is that the resources that I'll show you to help you find moats contain financial information; dollar amounts and terminology like cash flow, revenue, income. These are basic accounting terms, and even if you haven't taken an accounting course you can find their definitions through a quick search.

It might seem daunting at first, but don't expect to understand everything right away. Learn a little at a time, and over the course of a few weeks, months, and years, your knowledge will compound.

The two resources I think will help you find businesses with moats are *Value Line* and *Morningstar Premium*, which are described in the previous chapter. I have access to databases of both services through my local library in Seattle. You may want to check if your own library provides similar access. If they don't you can subscribe to either service on a monthly or annual basis. Before you do that, do check your local library because I imagine many libraries do subscribe to these materials and you won't know until you ask.

Value Line provides an in-depth analysis of individual companies, and in my opinion they provide the most useful set of numbers for stocks in America. You can use their guides as a quick summary of any company you're interested in to quickly measure one business against another.

Morningstar premium provides analyst commentary, financial information, and moat ratings: none, narrow, wide. You can filter all companies in their database to filter to see if a moat exists for the company you're considering. Their database does not provide the moat ratings for all companies, so think of it as a good starting point.

Billionaire investor Charlie Munger agrees that the Value Line summaries are the way to go — especially if you're not inclined to start reading annual reports.

I think the set of numbers the one set of numbers in America that are the best quick guide measuring one business against another are the *Value Line* numbers—that stuff on the log scale paper going back 15 years that is the best one-shot description of a lot of big businesses that exists in America. I can't imagine anybody being in the investment business involving common stocks without that thing on the shelf.

CHARLIE MUNGER

I think that *Value Line* is the best quick guide to financial numbers that you can find, and they will help you to figure out if a company has a moat. Often the company summary will not spell out that a company has a moat, but they will use words like "has an enduring advantage" or "far ahead of competition" and if you find enough instances of reading about a company being head and shoulders above the competition, they probably have a moat. Try to read about a several companies in the same industry, and before long you will get a sense of which one is the dominant player; that's the one with the moat.

Just as you've probably already noticed that Nike is the king of athletic apparel with a wide moat, followed by companies like Adidas and Under Armour, which possesses no moat. Under Armour is struggling to survive on many levels due to its lack of any durable competitive advantages. The more you learn about a few different companies in a given industry you'll start to figure out which ones are going to dominate, and which will always be struggling to stay alive.

Buffett said that you need to keep framework in your head of different industries and businesses. Once you know how the numbers look with different types of businesses, then you will have a backdrop upon which to measure new opportunities.

I mean, you know, if you'd never watched a baseball game and never seen a statistic on it you wouldn't know whether a .300 hitter was a good hitter or not. You have to have some kind of a mosaic there that your thinking is implanted against, in effect, and the *Value Line* figures, you know, they cycle it every 13 weeks, and if you ripple through that you'll have a pretty good idea of what's happened over time in American business.

WARREN BUFFETT

Moats are a powerful investing filter because they help you rule out many companies. You can just discard all kinds of sketchy businesses that might not even be alive in 10 years and focus on those durable companies that will likely dominate for years to come. If you are decisive on just a few outstanding wide-moat companies you can just seize the few opportunities that come your way in your lifetime.

This is not the attitude that they have at big investment advisers and mutual funds. They think if they study a million things they can know a million things. The result is that practically none of them can outperform the S&P 500 index...because these companies are so large, they essentially *are* the index.

Munger knows that doing less and knowing a few things well is better than studying a million things.[21] "I sit here with my Daily Journal stock, my Berkshire Hathaway Stock, my holdings in Li Liu's Asian Fund, my Costco stock, and of course I'm outperforming everybody, and I'm 95 years old, and I practically never have a transaction. And the answer is *I'm right and they're wrong*. And that's why it's worked for me and not for them."

The lesson to learn from Charlie Munger is that you succeed with just a few great stocks. One of the keys is to make sure that the companies you invest in have a moat — a durable competitive advantage.

Proof of how this works is the fact that almost all of Munger's billions are invested in just a few stocks. And you can ask "Why has this happened?" and the answer is pretty simple. "We tried to do less," Munger said. "We never had the illusion we could just hire a bunch of bright young people and they would know more about canned soup and aerospace and utilities and so on. We never had that dream.

We never thought we could get really useful information on all subjects like Jim Cramer pretends to have.

CHARLIE MUNGER

If you take nothing else from these pages, just realize that if you work really hard you can find a few things where you are right. A few things are enough; that's a realistic expectation.

TEN

S - SENSIBLE PRICE

EVERYBODY WANTS to buy stock at a cheap price. Yet for every person who buys someone is selling, and one of those people winds up being on a better side of every trade.

You can stack the odds in your favor by avoiding making stupid mistakes. This is easier said than done, but I want to tell you that from my own personal experience, I have sometimes succeeded and sometimes failed when trying to get a cheap price when buying a stock.

Waiting for a sensible price is not always good

To begin, I would say that one of the biggest mistakes I've made have been errors of "omission" rather than errors of "commission." I have lived in Seattle for 20 years, and I've seen companies like Amazon, Microsoft and Starbucks rise to prominence before my eyes. Microsoft's rapid growth phase had already happened when I started investing so I was late to that party.

Yet the Amazon story unfolded before my eyes. It was not always obvious that the company would dominate in so many different industries and have so much success in retailing, cloud computing, and many new areas the company continues to enter. I would say that in 2015 I was very clear that Amazon was an amazing company. I was already a member of its "Prime" loyalty program that offers expedited shipping, and I bought things from Amazon all the time. Yet the price was in the $500 range and seemed too expensive. I must have thought that it would drop to $250 or something and I'd have a better "entry point." As we know, that never happened.

So the lesson I have learned, and I would like to share with you is this: if you understand a company well, and use its services or products and many of your friends or family do too - don't wait too long. Sometimes sucking your thumb about a purchase decision can be a painful experience, and then years later you're left with regret.

A better plan might be to make sure you don't miss out on buying the stock altogether, and just buy a small amount of stock. You don't have to invest all of your money in that company at one time, but you can get started with a small purchase.

The interesting side-effect of buying a small position in a stock is that it causes you to pay more attention to it because you have "skin in the game" and then you'll be better informed and more aware of the company so you can make additional investments in the future if the company's prospects remain bright.

The Amazon example above explains what happens when you want to buy the stock of a growing company whose price climbs with few instances of going down so you can "buy on the dip." However, for the patient investor, there are usually brief, and sometimes prolonged periods of time in which the stock price falls or the entire stock market declines and these are valuable opportunities for the prepared investor with money ready to invest in their brokerage account.

Waiting for a sensible price can pay off

As far as a successful investment goes, I've long been a fan of

Berkshire Hathaway and bought some of the stock more than 10 years ago. I wanted to buy some more shares, but the company had performed well and in 2015 the stock was selling for about $140 a share. I had money saved to invest in the company, and I wanted to see if I could buy below $130 a share.

After waiting for what seemed like an eternity, in January of 2016 stock markets started to fall because of short-term fears about the economy. One day I watched attentively as the share price for Berkshire "B" shares fell to $125 a share. I had been hoping and preparing for a low price and acted decisively when the opportunity arrived. I believe that successful investors combine patience with decisiveness.

I believe that Benjamin Graham's advice to never buy after a substantial rise generally makes a lot of sense. However, with stocks of growing companies like Amazon, which has been on a substantial rise for many years (because the company has been growing for several years and the stock price mirrors this growth) not buying after a substantial rise can keep you from ever buying the stock.

With regard to the first part of Benjamin Graham's quote above, in the case of the Berkshire example above, you can see the value of not buying right after a substantial rise in the stock price; one day the market might drop and provide a much lower entry price.

The second part of Graham's advice — not selling after a substantial drop — is much easier to do, in my opinion. It doesn't require you wait and hope that stock prices fall. All you have to do is resist the urge to sell when the market declines. For me this is easy, because I not only resist the urge to sell, I'm waiting for the market to drop so I can buy more shares on the cheap. As Buffett says, "Be fearful when others are greedy, and greedy when others are fearful."

How to determine a sensible price

I'd like to show you simple way of determining the sensible price to pay for a stock.

There are a few steps involved because I wanted to break this down into small actionable items. There is some math included as well, but don't be scared off by it. It's not complicated, there are no formulas to memorize.

1. You need to determine a "sensible price" per share for the company you're considering for investment. To do this you need to take a step back and form an opinion about what the whole company is worth — you were a private buyer and buying the company in its entirely[1]. This next piece of advice is important: *Try not to look at the company's stock price* before doing this calculation; it may bias your decision.

For this example, let's use the Disney Corporation. Through my initial research, I learned that Disney owns:

Mickey Mouse
Frozen
Star Wars
Marvel
Pixar
ABC
ESPN
12 Theme Parks, 51 Resorts, 387 stores
195,000 employees
$55 billion in revenues
...Among other assets[2]

After all of my reading (annual reports, news articles) to gain a better understanding the different businesses that Disney owns, I decided that I'd pay $220 billion for the entire Disney company if it were for sale.

2. Next, I need to determine the number of outstanding shares (that just means number of shares that are available. It's easy to find this number: just do an online search using the company's name and the words "outstanding shares." For my example, I just searched for "Disney Corporation outstanding shares" and found the total listed as 1,800,000,000 shares.

3. Divide the dollar amount from #1 by the outstanding share number from step #2. The math looks like this: $275,000,000,000 / 1,800,000,000 = $152.78 dollars per share. That is the amount you consider a "sensible price" to buy the company on a "per share" basis.

4. Now that you've decided on your own (unbiased by the quoted price) you can take a look at current price quote for Disney stock, which, as of September 20th, 2019, is $132.27. The company is actually selling at a price far below what I would pay for the entire business; less than what I deem a "sensible price," the "S" in the PALMS filter.

5. In the example above, if you bought Disney stock at $132.27 you would be paying on a "per share" basis to buy Disney stock represents a 13% discount from your estimated value of $152.78. This discount can also be referred to as a "margin of safety[3]" and it protects you from errors in calculating intrinsic value or worse than average luck. A 13% discount is a decent margin of safety in case you make an error in your math or have worse than average luck.

What if your math in step #1 is not accurate?

It is difficult for a beginning investor to form an accurate opinion on the value of a company. There are analysts on Wall Street who spend 40-80 hours a week studying just one company, or a few companies, and their research is detailed. That does not mean that their understanding of a company is better than yours, but I'm just illustrating the fact that valuing a company takes time, and you should not expect at the outset to be able to quickly figure out a company's value.

In fact, I don't think it's possible to pinpoint an exact dollar value that a company is worth. It's more realistic to come up with a range of values that you estimate a company might be worth. For this exercise, you have to start with a number, so you can just pick a dollar amount somewhere in the middle of your range. It will help you to get started.

You might be wondering at this point, what if your calculations in step #1 were not accurate? What if the company is not really worth as much as you thought? Well, you have a margin of safety, and as long as it exists, you can make sure you are not paying a lot more than the quoted price. To be specific, if the company was actually worth $260 billion (and you mistakenly calculated it was worth $275 billion) the actual "sensible price" per share would be:

$260,000,000,000 (actual company value) / 1,800,000,000 (outstanding shares)[4] = $144.44/share

The current price quote for of $132.27 for Disney Stock (as of September 20, 2019) represents an 8.5% discount from $144.44, so even if the intrinsic value of the company is $260 billion instead of $275 billion, the margin of safety protects you from worse than average luck, because buying at $132.27 is still below $144.44 per share. According to your estimates of sensible price, you're still getting a discount if you can buy Disney at $132.27. That is the sensible price you arrived on your own before you checked the stock price.

I can't emphasize enough the importance of trying to figure out what the company is worth on your own, before looking at the stock price. I know you may glance at it, and I understand that you probably have an idea of what a stock is selling for when you start thinking about it.

But, if you take a little time to review the earlier chapter "Pay a Sensible Price" about not overpaying for Unicorn Stocks, and if you pay attention to coming up with a dollar amount that you'd pay for the entire business if you were a private buyer, then divide that by the shares outstanding, you will be well on your way to some advance, ninja-like investment work. You will truly be thinking for yourself and reducing the chances for making the easy mistake of overpaying.

Disclaimer: *Just as a reminder, all stock prices listed in this book are used to illustrate investing concepts. None of these prices suggest an opinion on companies mentioned, the direction of stock prices or the stock market in general.*

. . .

Company without a sensible price

There will be times you want to buy a stock, and you're working through the PALMS filter and you've been able to come up with a sensible read on every number except for price. I want to give you an example of a company that in my estimation passes on P, A, L, M, and you get stuck on the S for "Sensible Price." I would like to show you an example of a company that passes all but the last PALMS filters — so you can see what it looks like.

Let's look at Costco:

Profitable: Yes. Costco is profitable. You can check the income statement for proof.

Adaptable: Yes. Costco continues to innovate and thrive despite intense competition from Amazon and Walmart.

Loyal: Yes. Costco has a loyal customer membership base with strong traffic and 90% US membership renewal rates.

Moat: Yes. Costco has a wide moat that allows Costco to grow market share despite intense competition.

Sensible Price: No. The stock market is currently pricing in too much optimism for Costco's shares.

The price is the only factor that keeps Costco from looking like a great investment candidate.

As of September 20, 2019 Costco's stock is currently selling for 286.36/share.[5] In my estimation, a sensible price for these shares is closer to $220/share. As of August 2019 there were 444,000,000 shares outstanding[6].

Stock Price: $286.36 x 444,000,000 (shares outstanding) = $127,143,840,000 total company value

Let's see how much less you would pay for the entire business if the stock price were to decline to $220/share

Sensible Price: $220 (if stock price declines) x 444,000,000 (shares outstanding) = $97,680,000,000 for the entire business

As you can see, a decrease in stock price means you're getting the entire company (on a per-share basis) for much less money. There is always the chance that you will never see a lower price for Costco stock, so if you really want to buy the stock I would suggest that you heed Warren Buffett's advice, "It's far better to buy a wonderful company at a fair price than a fair company at a wonderful price." In my view, Costco is a wonderful company and the price is close to fair (perhaps only a little expensive) so if you plan on holding these shares for 5-10 years then you can always buy some shares now and wait to see if you can get a lower price for future share purchases.

A problem with Wall Street analysts

Many Wall Street analysts are good at analyzing numbers, but they put too much emphasis on financial math. In order to understand a business or an industry you have to bring your own understanding of the world, and the company into the picture. You can get fooled by fake numbers (some companies release data that is inaccurate, and various accounting tricks can make analysts see everything through "rose colored glasses").

You have an advantage if you use what you already know about a business as a starting point, rather than rely mainly on financial data that analysts consider. Use financial information as one of many tools, but don't rely on it too heavily or use data as your sole source of company information.

"Never buy a stock immediately after a substantial rise or sell one immediately after a substantial drop."

BEN GRAHAM

Don't buy stock after a big price run-up

It's hard not to buy a stock when it's getting bid up in value day after day, the company is in the headlines and you want to get rich along with everyone else. Remember that getting rich at investing should not be so easy. If it were, everyone would be rich.

Keep in mind that group behavior is often harmful to investors. It feels comfortable at the time, but that's because it's comfortable to buy things when they keep going up in price. You will do better investing when it's *least* comfortable, because people are fearful and they're selling. I know, it's counterintuitive, but remember that low prices are what you want to find, and sometimes you have to wait a long time for these opportunities to arrive. You just want to be ready for them. Here are a few tips to get in the right mindset to invest for the long-term.

1. Remind yourself that you are investing in a company. As Benjamin Graham said in his book, *The Intelligent Investor*, "A stock is not just a ticker symbol or an electronic blip; it is an ownership interest in an actual business, with an underlying value that does not depend on its share price."

2. Ask yourself "Would I be happy owning this company for the next 5 to 10 years?" Only buy if your answer is "yes."

3. Look up the currently quoted price for the stock. Is it at or near a 52-week high? If the answer is "yes," then wait for the price to fall. Try not to buy at the all-time high.

This approach will ensure you don't pay the "highest price" ever for the stock. The problem with this approach is that if the stock price never declines, you may never buy the stock.

Seth Klarman, a respected value investor, explained the benefits of buying stock at a low price. "We all know that the evidence shows that when you enter at a low price, you will have good returns, and when you enter at a high valuation, you will have poor returns," Klarman said. "Avoiding round trips and short-term devastation enables you to be around for the long term."[7]

. . .

It's good to have stock prices go nowhere for a while

Warren Buffett made this observation in 1963:

"...Our business is one requiring patience. It has little in common with a portfolio of high-flying glamour stocks...It is to our advantage to have securities do nothing price wise for months, or perhaps years, while we are buying them. This points up the need to measure our results over an adequate period of time. We suggest three years as a minimum..."

What if you want to buy an expensive stock?

This is a problem for investors who want to buy stocks at low prices; the stocks of many great companies today have been going up and up for many years, and to the casual observer it seems that their stock prices may never go down to a low price. People are very excited about the future of companies like Amazon, Apple, Facebook, Google, Netflix and others, and they are all piling in to these stocks, paying more and more to own them and in the process, driving the prices even higher.

Just because others are buying stocks does not mean you should too. Try to separate your desire to own part of a company from your fear of missing out on buying hot stocks. Warren Buffett expresses this sentiment as follows.

The line separating investment and speculation, which is never bright and clear, becomes blurred still further when most market participants have recently enjoyed triumphs," he said. "Nothing sedates rationality like large doses of effortless money. After a heady experience of that kind, normally sensible people drift into behavior akin to that of Cinderella at the ball. They know that overstaying the festivities — that is, continuing to speculate in companies that have gigantic valuations relative to the cash they are likely to generate in the future — will eventually bring on pumpkins and mice. But they nevertheless hate to miss a single minute of what is one helluva party. Therefore, the giddy participants all plan to leave just seconds before midnight.

There's a problem, though: They are dancing in a room in which the clocks have no hands.

BERKSHIRE HATHAWAY 2000 ANNUAL REPORT

So, you have a few choices here: you can avoid completely any investment where the price may be too high and steer clear of anything that could possibly be considered a speculation. Benjamin Graham offers a solution for times when you want to buy stock but the price seems to suggest that buying is more of a speculation (a gamble) rather buying at a sensible price.

Benjamin Graham offers a solution

If the price for a stock you want to buy seems a little too high — it's beyond what you deem sensible, can you "bend the rules" or add flexibility to your filtering system?

I say yes, you can do it, but you should be aware you are doing it. Say to yourself, "I think this stock is more expensive than a sensible investor would pay, and as a way to own a share of this company, I'm speculating a bit." This seems to me a sound approach to intelligent speculation. It lets you make an investment at a slightly higher price than you'd ordinarily pay without the risk that you'll make a mistake of omission and regret never getting a low enough entry price to buy the stock.

Graham doesn't say not to speculate, but rather he says you be intentional about it. Don't confuse it in your mind or try to convince yourself that you're investing when you're really just speculating.

Speculation is always fascinating, and it can be a lot of fun while you are ahead of the game. If you want to try your luck at it, put aside a portion – the smaller the better – of your capital in a separate fund for this purpose. Never add more money to this account just because the market has gone up and profits are rolling in. Never mingle your speculative and investment operations in the same account, nor in any part of your thinking.

BENJAMIN GRAHAM

By giving yourself this flexibility on price you open up the chance of buying shares of a fast-growing company, whereas if you waited for a price decline you may never buy it. As added insurance against paying too high a price, you can always start with a small initial investment, and if the stock declines substantially afterwards you can buy more shares.

Final thoughts about paying a sensible price

Investing is an art that requires creative thinking and imagination.

If math skills ensured investing success, then mathematicians could easily become rich.

Having good math skills and applying them to reading financial reports will not make you a good investor. Math and numbers are only one tool — and a small one at that, when it comes to investing. Some of the best investments are made with just a simple under-standing and a story you can tell about a company in a few sentences.

This is why the PALMS filtering system is a useful tool; it provides a multidisciplinary framework that requires some qualitative decision-making that you simply can't do with math alone. When you combine several different factors — profitability, adaptability, loyalty, moat and sensible price — you get a more robust mosaic of the company that lends to your "seeing" a more complete picture.

Each of the PALMS filters require research and reflection, and your ability to keep track of different items in your head and assemble them in a thoughtful way to tell a story about the company is a creative process. No two people will understand a company in exactly the same way.

At the end of the day, a company may pass every filter except the sensible price. If you believe the company makes sense on all other criteria except price, considering "paying up" for quality. You may pay more than you want initially, but if it's a great company and you hold for the long term, your investment could go up 100%, 300%, 500% or more.

If you feel confident in every other part of your reasoning, you may want to go ahead and buy a stock that seems expensive. You can always start by buying a small amount, and add more later. This way you will avoid mistakes of omission (you wait for years and never buy as the company grows and the stock price goes up. You can minimize your regret by buying stock in a company, even if it seems a bit expensive. Great companies are seldom cheap because other investors recognize their potential, and, like you, are willing to pay a premium for them.

Stocks won't be expensive all the time. If you wait, there are market dislocations every 5 years or so. To the patient investor, this can provide opportunities. Earlier in this book we learned how Ted Williams waited for the right pitch. In the same way, a successful investor waits for the right stock at the right price.

"What's nice about investing is you don't have to swing at every pitch. You can watch pitches come in one inch above or one inch below your navel, and you don't have to swing. No umpire is going to call you out." You get in trouble, Buffett says, when you listen to the crowd chanting "Swing, batter, swing![8]"

WARREN BUFFETT

Finally, you must have confidence in your facts and your reasoning.

"You're neither right nor wrong because other people agree with you. You're right because your facts are right and your reasoning is right—and that's the only thing that makes you right. And if your facts and reasoning are right, you don't have to worry about anybody else.

BENJAMIN GRAHAM

A final thought about paying a sensible price. You must be patient because just because you want to invest right now, it doesn't mean that prices are sensible (or cheap). At the time of this writing, stocks have been going up in price for the past 10 years without a serious drop in prices. I would say that it's highly likely that while prices are not entirely overpriced, they are not cheap either.

Keep in mind that super successful investors like Warren Buffett and Charlie Munger, and many others became rich because they were investing at times when stock sold at enormous discounts. Stocks basically went nowhere between 1966 and 1982, even though there was volatility in those times. Many smart investors took advantage of these very low prices for stocks and bought heavily then. Those low purchase prices are what contributed to their phenomenal returns in the decades that followed.

At the time of this writing, stocks are not selling at low prices by any stretch of the imagination. There are few areas of the market, perhaps with a few exceptions, that anyone could say are sensibly priced. However, for the patient investor, there will be opportunities to buy stocks when markets become irrational and investors are fearful. It's impossible to predict when this will happen, but those who buy stocks when they eventually become cheap will be the investors who get rich when stocks eventually recover.

Dollar bill shirt folded and photographed by the author

Many people get so excited to buy stock that they don't realize the price they pay has an enormous impact on their future returns.

I will tell you now that some of my best investments were total luck. I didn't know anything except that I liked the companies and stock price had little significance. I was fortunate enough to be able to invest in great businesses, such as Berkshire Hathaway, Carmax, and Waters, but that was more because of opportune timing than investment savvy on my part.

Later, I got excited about a few other companies, and again I bought in when I had the money. This time, though, I paid too much, and because my purchase price was so high, when I eventually sold many years later I had made no money on my investment. It was better than a loss, sure, but it was still a waste of time. Had I been more patient, I could have avoided this very preventable mistake.

You will find that as you invest, sometimes you will buy at a good price and sometimes you will pay too much. Your goal should be to try to be consistently patient and wait for opportunities to arise. These generally come when the stock market is cratering and everyone is scared. It's also the most difficult time emotionally to buy stocks, but it can be the most rewarding financially.

The one great piece of advice to take away here is to be patient and always have some cash on hand so you are prepared to take advantage of market crashes — which will definitely occur throughout your investing lifetime.

Charlie Munger explains why waiting is so hard:

"You have to be very patient, you have to wait until something comes along, which, at the price you're paying, is easy. That's contrary to human nature, just to sit there all day long doing nothing, waiting. It's easy for us, we have a lot of other things to do. But for an ordinary person, can you imagine just sitting for five years doing nothing? You don't feel active, you don't feel useful, so you do something stupid."

Buying stock near its all-time high is a disaster and you may never recoup your funds. I know people who bought Tesla a couple of years ago when it was at its all-time high. The excitement was so intense that everyone who loved the car (which I totally understand) got exuberant about the stock (a rookie mistake, Cotton, you hate to see it).

Everybody getting excited about a stock should be a warning to you. It can keep you out of trouble, and out of the horrible kind of value-destroying decisions that leave you with less money and more regret.

The following paragraph has the most "on target" ideas about finding "a sensible price" that I can hope to give you. As you learn and experience more about investing, remember these simple concepts:

As stock prices rise, the odds start turning against investors. When stock prices fall, the odds begin to work in your favor.

If you stay fully invested in the stock market when it rises, you won't have any cash to invest with when the market crashes.

It doesn't matter how cheaply you can buy great businesses when the market crashes, if you don't have cash on hand you're never going to make money.

If you can keep cash on the sidelines and not invest it all when the stock market rises, you'll be rewarded with fantastic long-term returns.

There is no way to know exactly what price you should pay, but if you follow the stock for a while you will likely find brief moments when a company has earnings that cause the stock to fall. Or there could even be external economic or political factors that provide you with a golden opportunity to buy stock at a sensible price. Make sure you're prepared by having a firm understanding of the company, and then do nothing but sit back, crack open a cold one, and wait. And wait.

Intrinsic Value

Keep in mind that *price is one thing,* and *intrinsic value* is another. Sometimes the price accurately reflects the value of the item purchased, and sometimes it doesn't. One thing's for sure: the price you pay has an enormous impact on future returns. Here's an example: say you want to bring home a pint of Ben & Jerry's ice cream and you go to the store. You probably already have an idea of what it will cost right now. My guess is the range is between $3 - $5.50 depending on whether it's on sale and where you buy it. Now what if you stopped by a store for ice cream and it cost $10 for that same pint? How about $20? You wouldn't buy it (I'm guessing, but maybe if you were really craving ice cream). You'd just say no and go to some other store. This is because you know, based on your extensive, life-long ice cream buying experience, that the *intrinsic value* of a pint of delicious ice cream is five bucks or less.

The same goes for donuts. You know that the *intrinsic value* of a basic donut these days is about $1 and if you go to a fancy donut cafe you might pay $2.50 or more for a donut with special toppings. But if someone tried selling you a $10 donut you wouldn't do it.

Now what's going on in the stock market *right now* is that the stock market is offering $20 pints of ice cream and $10 donuts. The *prices* of some stocks are too high and decoupled from the *intrinsic value* of the company. This makes no sense at all. In some cases (I'm talking Uber, Lyft, Tesla, Beyond Meat, and many others) these companies are selling stuff but not making a profit. In other words, they're *losing money* and have negative intrinsic value, but investors are paying inflated prices because they have dreams of a bright future. That's not investing, that's speculation. That's like paying $30 for a donut because you think you can sell it to someone else for more in the future. This party will end poorly...lots of expensive donuts and nobody to buy them. That's what stock market crashes do...they bring overpriced stock shares back to earth. It's nature's tough love way of saying "get real, stock market, you're dreaming!"

If you want better than average returns, pay attention to the price you pay and the intrinsic value of what you get in return. In this chapter we will look at ways to determine what a company is worth in its entirety, and what the price per share should be for its stock. We will then compare this to the market price of the stock to see if it's selling for a sensible price.

Let's Take a Look at Starbucks

I made a YouTube video a while ago in which I did a simple math problem to find out how I would value the company's stock. I made the YouTube video on August 21, 2017[9] and here are the numbers I used for the valuation.

1. Dollar amount I would pay if I were a private buyer and going to buy the entire Starbucks company: $80,000,000,000
2. Starbucks shares outstanding: 1,440,000,000
3. $80,000,000,000 ÷ 1,440,000,000 = $55.55 per share

The stock price for Starbucks (ticker symbol SBUX) at market close on 8/18/2017 was $52.70.

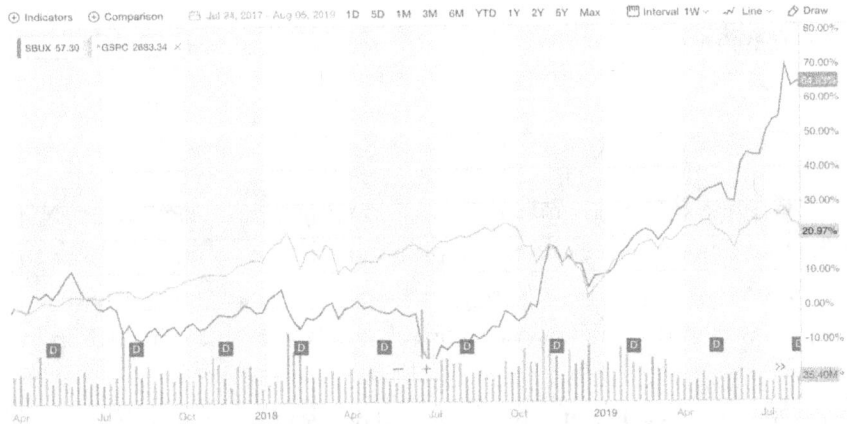

Starbucks Coffee Company stock price. The stock price remained well below the intrinsic value of the company for a long time before the market finally realized its value. Stock chart from Yahoo Finance

So, the $55.55 per share calculation of what Starbucks' business was worth was actually more than the closing price of $52.70. In my estimation, the market was undervaluing Starbuck's stock, and the stock was a good deal. This is the ideal situation you want to look for: the market's quoted price is less than your estimate of the company's intrinsic value.

Does Adobe sell at a sensible price?

I want to own stock in Adobe Corporation (ADBE). I understand it well, I use their products, and I want to buy it. But is the current stock price sensible in relation to the intrinsic value of the entire company?

Let's take a look. I do all of my research to understand the business, and I decide that if I would pay $125 billion for Adobe's entire business. Now I need to know how many shares are outstanding as of September 2019, and I Google "Adobe shares outstanding" and find that in Q3 2019 there are 490 million shares outstanding.

Quick math shows that $125,000,000,000 ÷ 490,000,000 shares = $254.58/share

So I've done this quick math without looking at the stock price. Now that I've done my back-of-the-napkin calculation of what I think the stock price *should* be, I Google the actual share price, which is $277.43[10]. So the stock is only about 8.2% "overvalued" based on my math.

Obviously if I were willing to pay more money — say $137 billion instead of $125 billion, then with the same number of shares outstanding, the price per share I'd be willing to pay would work out to $279.59 which is slightly more than the quoted price. Therefore, buying today at the quoted price would make sense. It wouldn't be "cheap" and give me a large margin of safety, but it would be a fair price and a good place to start.

But in reality, I would be willing to buy shares of Adobe at about $254.58. Just to be flexible in my thinking, I don't really want to only buy it at that exact price, because I might sit around waiting forever and it would not dip to exactly that dollar figure. I don't want to be sucking my thumb and never buy Adobe because the exact price I wanted was not delivered on a silver platter.

So, I set a price range that — if the stock price reached that range — I'd be comfortable buying the stock. I'd say anywhere around $250 a share or below would definitely catch my attention. $200 would be an excellent price to begin a position in Adobe.

The challenge for any investor

The challenge for any investor is estimating what the entire business is worth. There is no shortcut for this, and no way to look up the number. If you look at the stock price or market cap you're barking up the wrong tree, because these numbers are all based on market prices of the stock — and the market can both greatly overvalue and undervalue a business.

Your job is to identify these discrepancies, and you can only do this when you decide on the truth value of the company yourself. It takes time and effort to do your own research and come to an understanding, but be patient and learn as much as you can. As you can see in the Starbucks example above, it took quite a while for the market to realize that the business was worth more. The stock was cheap for a couple of years before the market noticed it was undervalued. This presented the patient investor with an excellent opportunity.

Now you might say, looking at the graph above, that an investor would have had to wait about two years for the market to recognize the value of Starbucks stock. That's true, and sometimes it takes longer. The economist John Maynard Keynes said, "The market can stay irrational longer than you can stay solvent." In the case of Starbucks, it was a relatively short time before the stock price started to climb, but sometimes this takes a long time.

Your goal should be not to buy stocks to try to make quick money, as short-term market fluctuations are impossible to accurately predict. As Buffett said, "If you aren't willing to own a stock for 10 years, don't even think about owning it for 10 minutes."

You get rich in the waiting

Your goal should be to try to be consistently patient and wait for opportunities. These generally come when the stock market is cratering and everyone is scared. It's also the most difficult time emotionally to buy stocks, but the most rewarding times financially. Rich people get that way by not going after every opportunity, but they wait for the few times that stocks get very cheap.

The one great piece of advice is to be patient and always have some cash on hand so you are prepared to take advantage of market crashes — which will definitely occur during your investing lifetime.

Charlie Munger explains why waiting is so hard:

"You have to be very patient, you have to wait until something comes along, which, at the price you're paying, is easy. That's contrary to human nature, just to sit there all day long doing nothing, waiting. It's easy for us, we have a lot of other things to do. But for an ordinary person, can you imagine just sitting for five years doing nothing? You don't feel active, you don't feel useful, so you do something stupid."

Buying stock near its all-time high can be a disaster from which you'll never recover. I know people who bought Tesla a couple of years ago when it was at its all-time high. The excitement was so intense that everyone who loved the car (which I totally understand) got exuberant about the stock (a rookie mistake) and people who bought anywhere between $350 and $385 in 2017 may never break even. It's actually possible that the stock was overpriced based on hopes and dreams, and those who overpaid may learn the lesson not to overpay the hard way.

Everybody getting excited about a stock should be a warning to you. It can keep you out of trouble, out of the horrible kind of value-destroying decision that leaves you with less money and more regret.

This next paragraph has the most "on target" ideas about finding "a sensible price" that I can give you. As you learn and experience more about investing, I believe you will remember these simple concepts:

- As stock prices rise, the odds start turning against

investors. When stock prices fall the odds start to work in your favor.

- If you stay fully invested in the stock market when it rises, you won't have any cash to invest with when the market crashes.
- It doesn't matter how cheaply you can buy great businesses when the market crashes, if you don't have cash you're never going to make money.

If you can keep cash on the sidelines and not invest it all when the stock market rises — if you can prepare with cash to buy stocks when they're cheap you you'll be rewarded with fantastic long-term returns.

There is no way to know exactly what price you should pay, but if you follow the stock for a while you will likely find brief moments when a company has earnings that cause the stock to fall, or economic or political factors provide you with opportunities to buy stock at a sensible price. Make sure you're prepared by understanding the company, and then do nothing but wait.

The nitty gritty of finding a sensible price

This is the secret that I seriously doubt many people use when deciding on what to pay for a stock. I share it with you because you deserve to know the best way to figure out a sensible stock price.

What I'm about to show you is simple. It doesn't take any math skills beyond those you learned in 5th grade, and you need only to search online for a couple of pieces of information and write them down, which should only take you a minute.

Once you understand this simple system you will be world-class in detecting sound prices and saying "no" to inflated prices.

Opportunity knocks

When stocks get cheap, sometimes the window of opportunity to buy is brief. I've seen stocks get cheap for a few days, and sometimes a week or two, but rarely longer than that. And this is often due to an unpredictable event; the company might have missed analyst-earning predictions, maybe the head of the Federal Reserve said something that spooked investors or perhaps a foreign country shot down a US plane.

When these kinds of events happen, a collective hysteria grips the stock market. Almost all stocks go down at the same time. Sometimes the losses are steep and sudden, sometimes they are gradual and prolonged. Whatever the cause, your friends, family, and co-workers will probably start talking about the dangers of the stock market. But these are the times when successful investing lifetimes are forged.

You must be prepared to buy the stock you've identified when the price becomes sensible, or if you're lucky, really, really cheap. All the waiting in the world is worthless if you don't have cash to deploy the moment you need it. You only have to act decisively.

You should be aware of the real possibility that stocks will drop a lot for whatever reason... and then continue to drop for weeks, months, or even years in a row. I have not experienced this happening for more than about 2-3 years at a stretch, but here are my words of caution to you: if the markets drop a lot, don't spend all of your investable money at once. Make sure to "keep some of your powder dry."

I have witnessed markets drop by 10% or 15% in a day, and that's when I happily bought some stock. A week later stocks dropped another 10%, and a month or two later another 20%. Market crashes are devious like that, they don't happen all at once, and they're often like prolonged, breathtaking plunges. And just when you think you've held on for dear life for the final drop, it falls again.

. . .

Be ready to buy at low prices

I like to have a few stocks that I'm thinking of buying on a list. I write their current price quote, and next to that the price at which I'd like to buy. I write this for a few stocks I'm considering, because if I follow five stocks there's a greater chance that one of them will decline by 10% or 20% than if I just focus on one stock. Make a "watch list" and stay focused on those stocks.

There are two ways I like stay up to date with stock prices so I'll know when a stock I'm considering drops in price: StocksTracker, and alerts available through any brokerage firm.

StocksTracker

I like the StocksTracker mobile app for following stocks. It's free and easy to follow stocks or create watch lists to follow a group of stocks. Another thing I like about the app is that you can see price changes in real time throughout the day.

Bear in mind, one thing I don't do is trade through the app. I only make watch lists that contain the stocks I'm considering buying while I wait to see if they drop by 10% or more.

Set email alerts via your brokerage app

There are many online brokerages that let you set alerts so that if a stock you're interested in buying drops by a certain dollar amount, or by a certain percent, it sends you an email. I have used alerts in the past and they are convenient.

In reality when I'm thinking of buying a stock I'm usually following the price from day to day, so I don't need the brokerage to send me an email; I know if the price has dropped and I'm ready to buy.

However, there are times when a stock drops unexpectedly and if you're at work or not paying attention it can be helpful to have an email alert hit your inbox to let you know about the price change.

. . .

Random dude from local Starbucks

I was at Starbucks talking with this guy named Bryan who I met a while back. He's kind of a Starbucks friend, we don't hang out elsewhere, but when we cross paths there we chat about random stuff. He dabbles in stocks, and he told me that lately he's trying to make money trading biotech stocks. You may know people like him, he invests in his free time, always trying to get rich quick jumping in and out of stocks, thinking he has an edge or knows what's going on. He owns about 20 stocks, all new investments, and he'll probably trade in and out of them, pretending that he's making money but probably losing because he doesn't have a businesslike approach or reliable system.

He and I talked about stocks, and since he's a trader it's clear we take a different approach. I take a business like approach and view buying a stock as buying part ownership in that business. I don't care if the stock market is open or closed today or tomorrow because I'm owning part of a business that I hope will grow its profits and return even more cash to me in 3, 5 or 10 years then it generates today. It's a very simple concept to understand.

Just so you'll know—I only own five stocks, and one of those stocks was a spin-off, I didn't even want it, but it's sitting in my account. So I only own four stocks that personally bought, and don't have plans to sell them any time soon. That is not a diversified portfolio, but they are outstanding companies and I'd rather add more money to those unless I find something better, which I haven't found in years.

He said something that is partly true, but I think it's based on short-term thinking. He told me that whenever he looks at Amazon's stock, it's always trading at its 52-week high. Apparently that has deterred him from buying the stock — the appearance that it is always expensive. It may appear that way because the stock price has been going up for years, but upon close examination there have been times when Amazon stock has gone on sale.

I don't know how closely he looked at Amazon's stock price, but I'm pretty sure he was giving his general feeling about Amazon being expensive, but not actually paying close attention to finding a sensible price. The graph below shows that Amazon declined from its highs and became less expensive. Any investor who was monitoring Amazon using the StocksTracker app or had set brokerage alerts to notify them when Amazon hit $1,400 or $1,300 would have been ready to buy that stock cheap relative to its earlier highs.

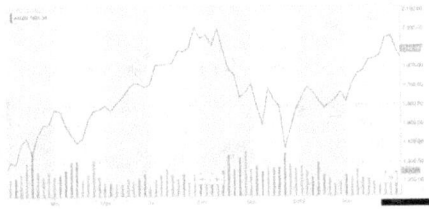

Amazon's stock price always seems to be high, yet there are times when prices fall unexpectedly and present low prices for prepared investors. During the fall and winter of 2018 Amazon's stock got cheap. This screenshot shows the graph of Amazon's stock price reaching $1,343.46 on December 24, 2018 — Christmas Eve. People waiting for Santa to come down the chimney could have picked up shares of Amazon on the cheap. Stock chart from Yahoo Finance.

If you look at the chart of Amazon's stock price in 2018 you'll see that while Amazon shares climbed from April through July, the stock price declined and there were opportunities for the investor who wanted to buy shares to do so in the 1400 range (and even the high 1300s late in the year).

The casual observer who says that a stock's price "is always too expensive" might not monitor the stock closely enough. If you aren't truly focused on the company and stock price why should you expect to take advantage of a rare opportunity? The alert investor will pick that ripe fruit from the tree at an opportune time and deserves the reward. The investor who casually glances up and says "nothing's ripe" may miss something.

I believe that the prepared mind that is decisive at the right moments can take advantage of market fluctuations and buy shares at a sensible price.

A sensible price for sure?

It's always hard to know at the moment you buy stock if you are paying "a sensible price" compared to what the stock may trade at in the future.

I don't think you should be too concerned about getting a precise price, but rather try to buy stock in a range that makes sense. All you have to go on is the historical prices for a stock, and they don't tell you anything. The right question to ask is whether it's a great company, and avoid buying it at it's all-time high. I prefer to wait for a stock to pull back on negative news about the company, which is often of a temporary nature, or news affecting the economy that will affect the stock market that day, week or month but that will usually blow over with time.

You never know until years have passed if you got a great entry price into a stock or you paid too much. You can tilt the odds in your favor by taking the advice of Benjamin Graham, who was the father of value investing and teacher and mentor to Warren Buffett.

"Never buy a stock immediately after a substantial rise or sell one immediately after a substantial drop," Graham said. When you're thinking of buying a stock, ask yourself if it's selling at its all-time high. It's natural for you (or anyone) to be most excited about buying a company when its stock price keeps going up. But keep in mind it's what they call "priced to perfection," which means the stock price assumes everything will be blue skies and apple pie. Any bad news about the company or economy can take that air out of the company in an instant, and the stock price can fall fast. Don't buy stock just because everyone else is buying. Buy stock because you understand the company and it's selling at a sensible price.

Also, make sure to spread your purchases out over time. You take a lot of risk if you buy in all at once because you could be buying everything at or near a price peak. Instead, if you have money to invest, buy stock in a few different trades over at least a year, and preferably a larger time frame. This way you reduce the risk of putting all your money to work and overpaying for stock.

Don't worry, nobody "knows" ahead of time that they price they are paying is low. Many "value" investors who specialize in buying cheap stocks, or those whose value they determine to be far greater than the price they pay...only to find that the price continues to decline, sometime for years.

Nobody knows the perfect price to buy any stock. The stock price on any given day is just the consensus on that given day based on all commonly known information about a company's financial condition and future prospects.

If you think about buying a quality business and holding for a long time you will be focusing on what's truly important. Picking the perfect price will be less crucial when you look at your decision five, 10 or 20 years later.

When to buy stocks

I like to buy stocks when the market crashes. I never worry about stock prices plunging, because I plan to invest for many years and I view every price decline in a business I love as a buying opportunity.

Even if the market does not crash 30% to 50% you can still get decent bargains during occasional market declines. As Charlie Munger said, "Successful investing requires this crazy combination of gumption and patience, and then being ready to pounce when the opportunity presents itself, because in this world opportunities just don't last very long."

You will do well if you can wait until a stock you understand has declined in price by 10% to 20%. Any time I see this kind of discount in the stock of an outstanding business I get ready to pounce. I think it makes sense to write down a price range that you want to buy at, and just be patient. You will be prepared if the stock eventually declines into the price range you set. Your willingness to buy stocks should increase as their prices fall.

ELEVEN

PUTTING IT ALL TOGETHER

WE WILL NOW PUT a few companies through the PALMS filtering system to see whether they pass.

I always find it exciting to learn about a new businesses because at the start I don't know about their product or service. At first you draw an outline, and then you fill in the details. Before long you'll have a complete picture.

I'm going to put three companies through the PALMS filter: Stone Company, a Brazilian payment processor, Bright Horizons, a network of child care centers, and Zoom Video Communications.

What's interesting about investing for the long-term is the quest is for large, established companies with a history of profitability. There is really no problem with this approach; it's reliable, you don't lose money, and if the company grows its earnings over time your ownership stake grows in value. It's really easy.

The one thing I see lacking from investing only in large companies is that once a company becomes dominant and established everyone other investor knows about it too. It has probably already had its rapid growth phase. Though the company may still have a bright future, you might not have been owning the shares when they doubled, and doubled again, etc.

Starbucks was a fast growing company about 20 years ago, and this rapid growth continued until recently. Now, while still growing, it's so large that it's hard to keep growing at the same rate. The larger you get, the harder it is to double or quadruple in size.

Three companies to run through the PALMS filter:

We will look at Bright Horizons, Stone Company & Zoom Video Communications. I'm going to give you a little background on the first two because you're already familiar with Zoom.

PALMS filter for Bright Horizons

Bright Horizons is a United States–based child-care provider and is the largest provider of employer-sponsored child care. It also provides back-up child care and elder care, tuition program management, education advising, and student loan repayment programs. It is headquartered in Watertown, Massachusetts.[1]

1. Profitable - Yes, the company had net income of $158 million for the FY2018[2].
2. Adaptable - It looks like Bright Horizons is adapting to new technology, for example the company leverages technology by using an online training program to provide formal education to its employees. The online program for the Child Development Associate (CDA) credential offers employees 120 hours of formal education and prepares them to file and gain their CDA credential.
3. Loyal - It seems as though not only are individuals bringing their children and infants to Bright Horizons for

car, but many companies are loyal to Bright Horizons and use them as a way to provide child and infant care services for their employees. Sprint, Target, General Mills, Salesforce and Allstate are mentioned among other loyal customers.

4. Moat - I do not think this company possesses an economic moat because in all likelihood it would be hard to create barriers to entry to a child care company. I do think their use of technology to provide training saves time and money, and the network of 1000+ child care centers and 32,000 employees across the globe will make it hard to hurt their business, but I don't think there is any way for them to prevent others from entering the same business. So any moat that could exist would not be a wide moat, it would be narrow or non-existent.

5. Sensible Price - The market capitalization for Bright Horizons is $8.7 billion and the revenues for FY2018 are $1.9 billion. This stock is selling for 4.6x revenues. That seems like a fair price, especially when compared to some other companies like Zoom which is selling for 73x revenues.

PALMS filter for Stone Company

Known in Brazil as Stone Pagamentos (Stone Payments), Stone Company is a Brazilian financial technology company founded in 2012, and it focuses on payment processing and financial services. The company offers e-commerce solutions (like PayPal or Square) and point of sale solutions like the "Square Registers" popular in retailers in the US. Stone Company is headquartered in Rio de Janeiro and São Paulo Brazil.

1. Profitable - I'm excited about this company and want to buy the stock, but I'm holding off right now. Not jumping in, patience.

2. Adaptable - In the offering prospectus, Stone claims to have more than 200,000 active customers in Brazil, and suggests that it will explore that distribution channel to offer other products and solutions. Stone says it's exploring "digital banking and specific vertical software solutions[3]."

3. Loyal - Stone claims to have more than 200,000 active customers in Brazil, and suggests that it will explore the distribution channel to offer other programs such as CRM solutions and loyalty programs.

4. Moat - Stone is a relatively new company and has competition in the form of PagSeguro in Brazil. However, while Stone grew up competing with the old duopoly formed by incumbents Rede and Cielo, PagSeguro created a niche market for itself: individual micro entrepreneurs (MEIs in the Brazilian Portuguese acronym). That niche is now being aggressively attacked by other players.[4]However, Stone has a proprietary distribution force that interacts directly with merchants. The size of the commercial staff is not disclosed, but these sales, service, and support teams reach out to customers directly through about 180 Stone Hubs throughout Brazil and let the company work directly to cement the company's relationship with customers. These hubs could provide a barrier to entry and make it harder for PagSeguro to compete with Stone.

5. Sensible Price - The market capitalization for The Stone Company is $10.1 billion and the revenues for FY2018 are $728 million. This stock is selling for 13.9x revenues. That seems like a sensible price, especially when

compared to some other companies like Zoom which is selling for 73x revenues.

PALMS filter for Zoom

Zoom Video Communications provides remote conferencing services using cloud computing. Zoom offers communications software that combines video conferencing, online meetings, chat, and mobile collaboration. It was founded in 2011 by Eric Yuan and is headquartered in San Jose, California

1. Profitable - Yes, the company earned a profit of $8 million in FY2018.
2. Adaptable - Yes, this company is rapidly adapting to new technologies as software is its core business.
3. Loyal - Everything I've learned about Zoom suggests that a loyal and devoted user base is central to its success. They are loyal because Zoom makes their video conferences frictionless. As loyal users spread the word about Zoom and more people find out about it, the company may experience widespread adoption and its marketing costs could decrease.
4. Moat - Zoom has steep competition from other tech companies like Skype (owned by Microsoft), Google, and possible future offerings from Amazon.com and Facebook. This company has no moat, so you'd have to be flexible and realize that if you're going to invest in a startup they won't be resistant to competition.
5. Sensible Price - At $82.63, Zoom's stock price is not sensible at all, but it could become a good buy if the stock price declined a lot. The market cap for Zoom Video Communications is $24.1 billion and the revenues for FY2018 are $331 million. This stock is selling for 73x

revenues, which is ridiculous. I think Zoom is a better
buy around $34 a share.

I hope that taking a closer look at Bright Horizons, Stone
Company and Zoom has been instructive. You need a simple system
to organize useful information about stocks. I hope you find these
simple filters are helpful to you too.

TWELVE

THE MAGIC BOX

Einstein is credited with saying compound interest is the most powerful force in the universe. The notion of putting money away is most important to the cohort that least understands it: young people.

SCOTT GALLOWAY

COMPOUND INTEREST IS the key to investing. It is very powerful, and it's hard to get. The problem with getting it is that it requires you to not only invest in stocks of wonderful companies, but also not destroying what you get by interrupting its force.

Charlie Munger puts it this way: "Understanding both the power of compound interest and the difficulty of getting it is the heart and soul of understanding a lot of things[1]," he said. I would add that starting the snowball at a young age and gradually letting it gain size over your lifetime is the key to harnessing its power.

Scott Galloway has a great YouTube video where he challenges viewers: "If I could give you a magic box and tell you that if you put a thousand dollars in that box at the age of 25, by the time you're 65 you can open that box and you would have between $15,000 and $25,000, how much would you put in the magic box?[2]"

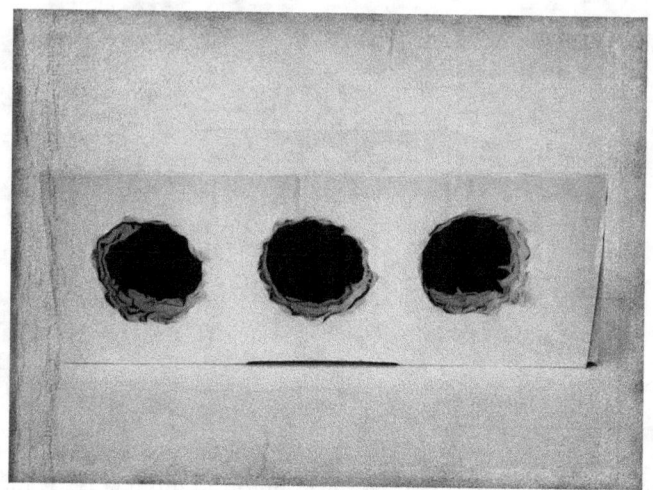

If you had this magic box and put $1,000 into it so that in 40 years it's $10,000 to $25,000, how much money would you put in it? Photo © Jeff Luke

Galloway says that "Most of us, when we're younger, believe that we're gonna the big win, we're gonna hit the home run and have a big liquidity event. Assume that won't happen."

Instead, he gives advice that I think is on point. I know because I started doing this myself many years ago. I made monthly investments into a mutual fund before I knew enough to buy stocks individually. It was easy to make it a monthly habit, and it paid off. "Pay yourself first every month force yourself to save a little bit of money," Galloway said. "Saving a little bit of money at a young age goes a long, long way in case you don't have that big liquidity event."

It's easy to fall into the trap of believing you can just spend all of your income because as you get older, you'll get more awesome and make more money. Keep optimistic about your future, but don't assume you'll get rich through ginormous paychecks or lottery winnings.

Don't just think about how much money you earn, thinking of how much you *burn*. Young people focus on how much money they earn, adults also focus on the other side of the ledger, and that is their burn.

What you want to aim for is having money coming in — passive income — that's greater than your burn. If you have $45,000 coming in a year, and you only spend $40,000, *you are rich*.

Compound Interest

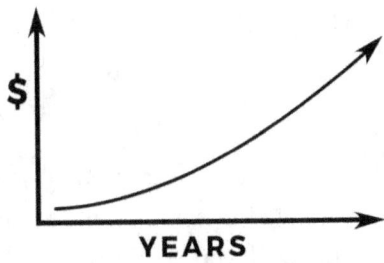

Einstein is credited with saying that compound interest is the most powerful force in the universe. Money invested today grows many times over in the future. Benjamin Franklin wrote, "Remember that money is of a prolific generating nature. Money can beget money, and its offspring can beget more, and so on."

How will you get to a point of true wealth and being rich? Look for ways that your passive income from stocks, dividends, or other assets can produce income that at some point that will be greater than your burn. But also figure out how you will get that burn to a manageable level such that what you earn will overtake what you burn sooner rather than later.

THIRTEEN

HOW TO READ AN ANNUAL REPORT

LEARNING to read the financial statement in an annual report — written in the language of business, which is accounting — is a lot like learning a foreign language. If you really want to have an advantage when reading financial documents, take an accounting class. If you've already taken one then you're already a step ahead.

But let's get real. I don't expect you to be so excited about numbers that you're going to follow me through this chapter and the next. There is important data that you can uncover in these financial statements, but you can also get them in other places like in *Value Line*. I find their one-page summaries invaluable in getting a quick summary of a company without having to dive into a company's accounts. I have a free subscription to *Value Line* that I can access on my city's library database. You might want to check to see if your library is subscribed to it too — it's a great resource.

You'll find it a lot easier to read through *Value Line* than looking at the assets and liabilities on a balance sheet, so if you've never read financial statement just start there because it's a piece of cake to read. It also gives you a few super useful pieces of information: a company's financial strength, which it rates 1 (best) - 5 (worst) and that lets you know how resilient a company is so you'll get an idea of how well it might survive a recession.

If you're like me, you might have an aversion with anything that sounds boring from the start. "Annual" sounds boring, and if that's not bad enough, it's got "report" after it. Reminds me of report cards, or TPS reports[1], or any host of mind-numbing things I'd prefer to avoid.

I will give you a free pass to skip this chapter and the next one about reading the K-1. I truly believe these two chapters will provide insanely useful info to those who want to dive deep into the finances that matter in a company, but I realize that not every investor wants to do this right now. So, feel free to skip ahead to the chapter titled, "Get Ready to Buy Stocks."

With that said, I do think the info in this chapter and the next one will help you really up your investing game. It will essentially put you in the "big leagues" with the financial analysts and master investors who read many reports a day and understand companies inside and out before investing.

It's true, you can buy stock in a company without ever reading the annual report (many people do) you will be much better off if you have a deep understanding of what the hell is going on in the company. The company's management uses the annual report, which is full of numbers, to explain everything about its business during the past year and its plans for the future.

It's no surprise why most annual reports get tossed right into the recycle bin. The text and colorful digital photos on glossy paper are nice on the eyes, but they teach you nothing. The numbers in the back are nearly impossible to understand, and they're supposed to be the most important part.

So what's an investor to do? Well, I want to show you how to get something out of an annual report in a few minutes, and that's all the time you need to spend with one. I'm going to lead you through an annual report and show you how exactly what you need to know to make sense of it.

Let's take a look at NVIDIA Corporation's 2018 Annual Report as the example. If you want to download it and follow along it just do a quick Internet search, download it, and follow along.

The annual report to shareholders

The annual report to shareholders is a small book (really a pamphlet), and it often has a glossy cover, photos, and includes a letter to shareholders from the CEO. The annual report is the company's one chance to communicate with shareholders during the year, and they put time and energy into making the report accurately express the financial condition of the company and what happened over the past year. Let's start by looking at the NVIDIA Corporation annual report.

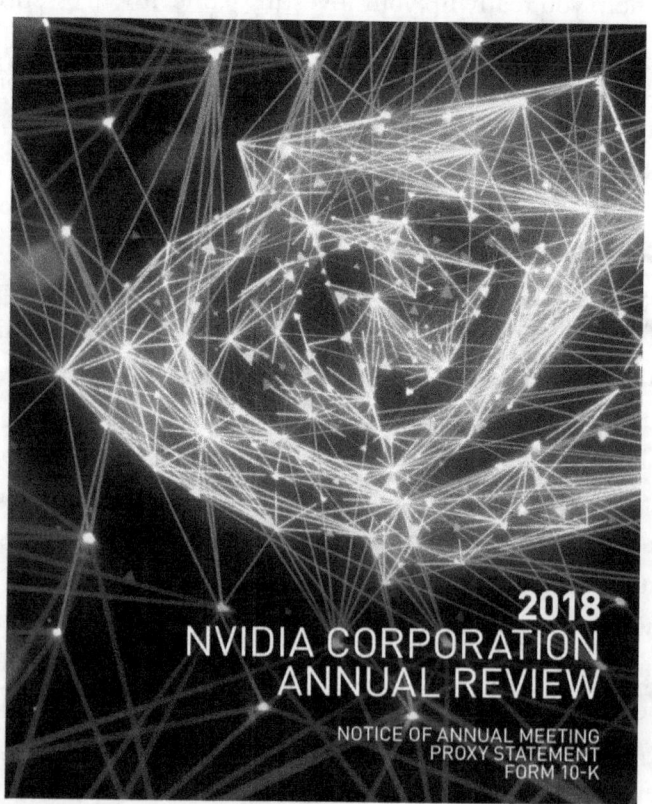

2018
NVIDIA CORPORATION
ANNUAL REVIEW

NOTICE OF ANNUAL MEETING
PROXY STATEMENT
FORM 10-K

Just to give you a little background, NVIDIA started out with a focus on PC graphics, and then invented the graphics processing unit, or GPU, to solve some of the most complex problems in computer science. In recent years they have extended their focus to artificial intelligence, or AI.

If you take a look at the 2018 NVIDIA annual report, you'll see it has a beautiful color image on the cover, and some inside are some pretty color pictures of scientists using GPU computing to see gravitational waves for the first time in human history, a photo taken by NVIDIA Ansel, a powerful in-game camera that lets users take photos of their games, and someone driving "hands-free" in a car that uses NVIDIA DRIVE PX Pegasus supercomputer the size of a license plate.

I breeze past all those photos and turn directly to the Consolidated Balance Sheet printed on page 43 of the report (see chart below). The balance sheet lists the assets and then the liabilities. Those are the two most important items to me and I'll show you why. First, let me tell you which numbers matter.

NVIDIA CORPORATION AND SUBSIDIARIES
CONSOLIDATED BALANCE SHEETS
(In millions, except par value)

	January 28, 2018	January 29, 2017
ASSETS		
Current assets:		
Cash and cash equivalents	$ 4,002	$ 1,766
Marketable securities	3,106	5,032
Accounts receivable, less allowances of $13 as of January 28, 2018 and January 29, 2017	1,265	826
Inventories	796	794
Prepaid expenses and other current assets	86	118
Total current assets	9,255	8,536
Property and equipment, net	997	521
Goodwill	618	618
Intangible assets, net	52	104
Other assets	319	62
Total assets	$ 11,241	$ 9,841
LIABILITIES, CONVERTIBLE DEBT CONVERSION OBLIGATION AND SHAREHOLDERS' EQUITY		
Current liabilities:		
Accounts payable	$ 596	$ 485
Accrued and other current liabilities	542	507
Convertible short-term debt	15	796
Total current liabilities	1,153	1,788
Long-term debt	1,985	1,983
Other long-term liabilities	632	277
Total liabilities	3,770	4,048
Commitments and contingencies - see Note 12		
Convertible debt conversion obligation	—	31
Shareholders' equity:		
Preferred stock, $.001 par value: 2 shares authorized; none issued	—	—
Common stock, $.001 par value: 2,000 shares authorized; 932 shares issued and 606 outstanding as of January 28, 2018; 868 shares issued and 585 outstanding as of January 29, 2017	1	1
Additional paid-in capital	5,351	4,708
Treasury stock, at cost (326 shares in 2018 and 283 shares in 2017)	(6,650)	(5,039)
Accumulated other comprehensive loss	(18)	(16)
Retained earnings	8,787	6,108
Total shareholders' equity	7,471	5,762
Total liabilities, convertible debt conversion obligation and shareholders' equity	$ 11,241	$ 9,841

The NVIDIA balance sheet. You can find and peruse this financial statement in less than a minute to see if a company whose stock you're thinking of buying has an improving or deteriorating balance sheet.

In the top column titled Current Assets, I notice that the company has $4.002 billion in cash and cash equivalents, plus $3.106 billion in marketable securities. Adding these two items together, I get the company's current overall cash position, which I round off to $7.11 billion. Comparing the 2017 cash to the 2018 cash in the right-hand column, I see that NVIDIA is socking away more and more cash. This is a sure sign of prosperity.

Then I go to the other half of the balance sheet, down to the entry that says "long-term debt." Here I see that the 2018 long-term debt is $1.985 billion, virtually unchanged from last year. Ultimately I like to see the long-term debt reduced, but it's okay if it remains the same; you just don't want it to increase too much.

Debt reduction is another sign of prosperity. When cash increases relative to debt, it's an improving balance sheet. When it's the other way around, it's a deteriorating balance sheet.

Subtracting the long-term debt from cash, I arrive at $5.12 billion , NVIDIA's "net cash" position. The cash and cash equivalents alone exceed the debt by $5.12 billion. When cash exceeds debt it's very favorable. No matter what happens, NVIDIA isn't about to go out of business.

You may have noticed NVIDIA's short-term debt of $15 million. I ignore short-term debt in my calculations. The purists can fret all they want about this, but why make things complicated? I assume that the company's other assets (inventories, etc.) are worth enough to cover the short-term debt, and I keep moving.

As often as not, it turns out that long-term debt exceeds cash, the cash has been shrinking and debt has been growing, and the company is in weak financial shape. That's a company you don't want to own. This exercise is just going to let you know if the company is weak or strong.

Next, I look at the first page of the 10-K and can see that the number of shares of NVIDIA common stock outstanding as of February 26, 2018 was 605 million.

Dividing the $5.12 billion in cash and cash equivalents by the 605 million shares outstanding, I conclude that there's $8.46 in net cash to go along with every share of NVIDIA. In some companies you may have a situation where the stock might be selling for $80 but there's $8.46 of cash to go along with every share. That means that the stock is actually cheaper — it's as thought the stock is trading closer to $81.50. With NVIDIA selling at $172.69[2] about 5% of the stock price is backed up by cash — money in the company to back up the shares. NVIDIA is not a deteriorating company that's saddled with debt. Having a lot of extra cash in the bank is always a good problem to have.

FOURTEEN

ANATOMY AND DISSECTION OF A 10-K

THE 10-K (or simply the "K[1]") is a packet of different financial reports that shows the financial condition of the company at year's end[2]. It describes the company's financial health, revenues, debts, and profits, and also risks to the business so investors can get a full-color picture of the company's financial condition during the past year[3].

Why read the 10-K?

You can travel to France and get by just fine without without speaking French. Sure, you can get away with speaking English most of the time with an occasional "bonjour," and "merci" thrown in, but your travels will be more rich and memorable if you speak French. We're not talking about being perfectly fluent, but having a basic conversation skills will make it so much easier to meet real Parisians and one day you'll find yourself with your new friends, sharing wine and a baguette along the banks of the Seine as the sun descends, or sharing a breakfast of coffee, croissants & fruit.

I know this can happen because when I was 27 I traveled through Europe by train, going from Paris to Barcelona to Lisbon and then Geneva, sometimes in a sleeper car in a train and other times staying in youth hostels, in farm yards, and in apartments in the city. In many places I became friendly with people who didn't speak English *because I knew their language.*

Just as you'll develop a more intimate connection to a culture when you understand their language, you can understand a company on a deep level if you're *familiar with the language of business: accounting.*

If the previous chapter about how to read an annual report was just enough working with financial numbers then please feel free to skip this chapter — you won't miss anything, and you won't fail as an investor! This chapter does give you some extra tools to "drill down" into a company's financial reports to see all of the moving parts of the business, but you don't have to know these details to succeed. I invested for many years without knowing what a 10-K was, and I did fine. I just wish I'd known how to read one, and I never found a book that explained it clearly, so I decided to write this book for you.

So for those of you who would rather sit in rush hour traffic on a hot day with no AC than read a bunch of numbers, I totally understand that, and you are forgiven in advance for skipping this chapter! It will be here for you later if you feel like returning to it. However, if you're one of those people who likes to get granular and dissect things to see how everything works, I'm going to show you how to dig into the 10-K to gain an understanding that few mortals will ever have about the company. You will truly be an expert.

Just for perspective, who actually reads these financial documents? Well, Warren Buffett happens to enjoy reading annual reports[4] from cover to cover and he reads every footnote. I'm sure it comes as no surprise that he's also the greatest living investor.

Financial analysts who work for brokerage firms like Goldman Sachs read annual reports because their job is to recommend stocks to brokers and their customers[5]. The analysts who work for mutual funds, pension funds, and universities like Harvard or Yale recommend stocks for their portfolio managers to buy[6].

So, as you can see, the people who make stock decisions that have a lot riding on them want to understand every detail of a business so they can see a little further into the future about potential new positive developments, and also to try and steer clear of any potential disasters. As a regular "small" investor who is in all likelihood not managing billions of dollars, you are not required to do the same reading as the professionals. But what if you had access to the same top secret information? What would you do with these superpowers?

Let's dive in and learn how to read a 10-K.

The 10-K

The language of business is accounting, so if you've already taken an accounting course you'll be especially well-equipped to read a 10-K. Have no fear, however, because if you haven't taken an accounting class you can still pick apart and understand a 10-K, and I'll show you how. I have never taken accounting, and I had to learn everything on my own. It takes time and watching a lot of videos, but it's all possible. I'm going to break down a year's worth of learning about reading a 10-K in the following pages.

If you're considering buying stock in a company at the moment, then I encourage you to download its 10-K right now. It will only take a minute to find and download it...I promise, it's really easy. Just search for the company name followed by the words "annual report." Once you start reading through the annual report you'll arrive at the 10-K.

If you just want to start reading the 10-K, then just type in the company name and 10-K. For example, we will look at Microsoft's 10-K together, so to find that document I Googled "Microsoft 10-K" and it was the first result. Easy peasy.

I promise you that the 10-K is not hard to understand. I will show you how to follow and learn from it.

How to read the 10-K

Keep in mind that every business is different and that will dictate the way you should read their specific annual report. What might be important to look at for an apparel company like Nike might be different than a tech company like Apple or an entertainment company like Disney, so be prepared to put on a different "thinking cap" for the variety of companies out there.

You don't want to end up missing something crucial to making an investment decision because you paid close attention to only the details I outline in this chapter. Keep in mind this is meant to give you a good overview, but I want to encourage you to spend as much time on any part of the 10-K as you want. I don't want you to miss out on any details crucial to your investment decisions.

So with that, here is a full breakdown of how I like to look through a 10-K for the first time, what's important to focus on, and what can be skipped over to save time and not fall asleep from boredom.

Business Description

The first part of the 10-K provides a description of the business. It doesn't matter how much I think I know about the business at the start, I always approach it like a total newbie because I want new eyes and go in pretending I don't know anything about it yet. So I'll skim the cover page to make sure I know where the headquarters are located, how many shares of the company are outstanding, what the market capitalization is, and when the fiscal (business) year ends. It's all basic stuff, but it's a good habit to peruse the basic description before you continue.

Perusing the Microsoft 2018 10-K (you can download it if you want to follow along) I see that aggregate market value of the company's common stock was $650.1 billion[7] and there were 7,668,217,316 shares of common stock outstanding. Right away something struck me: the current market value of Microsoft's common stock in September 2019 is $1.04 trillion, so in a short period of time the company's market value has increased more than $350 million. That's something I wouldn't have noticed without reading the business description.

UNITED STATES
SECURITIES AND EXCHANGE COMMISSION
Washington, D.C. 20549

FORM 10-K

☒ ANNUAL REPORT PURSUANT TO SECTION 13 OR 15(d) OF THE SECURITIES EXCHANGE ACT OF 1934

For the Fiscal Year Ended June 30, 2018

OR

☐ TRANSITION REPORT PURSUANT TO SECTION 13 OR 15(d) OF THE SECURITIES EXCHANGE ACT OF 1934

For the Transition Period From _____ to _____

Commission File Number 001-37845

MICROSOFT CORPORATION

WASHINGTON
(STATE OF INCORPORATION)

91-1144442
(I.R.S. ID)

ONE MICROSOFT WAY, REDMOND, WASHINGTON 98052-6399

(425) 882-8080

www.microsoft.com/investor

Securities registered pursuant to Section 12(b) of the Act:

COMMON STOCK, $0.00000625 par value per share   NASDAQ

Securities registered pursuant to Section 12(g) of the Act:

NONE

Indicate by check mark if the registrant is a well-known seasoned issuer, as defined in Rule 405 of the Securities Act. Yes ☒ No ☐

Indicate by check mark if the registrant is not required to file reports pursuant to Section 13 or Section 15(d) of the Exchange Act. Yes ☐ No ☒

Indicate by check mark whether the registrant (1) has filed all reports required to be filed by Section 13 or 15(d) of the Securities Exchange Act of 1934 during the preceding 12 months (or for such shorter period that the registrant was required to file such reports), and (2) has been subject to such filing requirements for the past 90 days. Yes ☒ No ☐

Indicate by check mark whether the registrant has submitted electronically and posted on its corporate website, if any, every Interactive Data File required to be submitted and posted pursuant to Rule 405 of Regulation S-T (§232.405 of this chapter) during the preceding 12 months (or for such shorter period that the registrant was required to submit and post such files). Yes ☒ No ☐

Indicate by check mark if disclosure of delinquent filers pursuant to Item 405 of Regulation S-K (§229.405 of this chapter) is not contained herein, and will not be contained, to the best of registrant's knowledge, in definitive proxy or information statements incorporated by reference in Part III of this Form 10-K or any amendment to this Form 10-K. ☐

Indicate by check mark whether the registrant is a large accelerated filer, an accelerated filer, a non-accelerated filer, a smaller reporting company, or an emerging growth company. See the definitions of "large accelerated filer," "accelerated filer," "smaller reporting company," and "emerging growth company" in Rule 12b-2 of the Exchange Act.

Large accelerated filer ☒

Accelerated filer ☐

Non-accelerated filer ☐ (Do not check if a smaller reporting company)

Smaller reporting company ☐

Emerging growth company ☐

If an emerging growth company, indicate by check mark if the registrant has elected not to use the extended transition period for complying with any new or revised financial accounting standards provided pursuant to Section 13(a) of the Exchange Act. ☐

Indicate by check mark whether the registrant is a shell company (as defined in Rule 12b-2 of the Exchange Act). Yes ☐ No ☒

As of December 31, 2017, the aggregate market value of the registrant's common stock held by non-affiliates of the registrant was $650.1 billion based on the closing sale price as reported on the NASDAQ National Market System. As of July 31, 2018, there were 7,668,217,316 shares of common stock outstanding.

DOCUMENTS INCORPORATED BY REFERENCE

Portions of the definitive Proxy Statement to be delivered to shareholders in connection with the Annual Meeting of Shareholders to be held on November 28, 2018 are incorporated by reference into Part III.

The first page of the Microsoft 10-K. There you have it, this might actually be the first time you've seen one of these documents. If you're thinking of buying stock in a company, I highly recommend downloading the 10-K and reading through it. Don't be intimidated, it's an important step in becoming an expert about the company.

The business description is the first part of every 10-K. You can check out the history of the business and any changes in the company's business segments. I have not carefully trained accounting training, yet it says it right there plain as day: "We operate our business and report our financial performance using three segments: Productivity and Business Processes, Intelligent Cloud, and More Personal Computing. Our segments provide management with a comprehensive financial view of our key businesses."

BUSINESS

GENERAL

Embracing Our Future

Microsoft is a technology company whose mission is to empower every person and every organization on the planet to achieve more. We strive to create local opportunity, growth, and impact in every country around the world. Our platforms and tools help drive small business productivity, large business competitiveness, and public-sector efficiency. They also support new startups, improve educational and health outcomes, and empower human ingenuity.

We continue to transform our business to lead in the new era of the intelligent cloud and intelligent edge. We bring technology and products together into experiences and solutions that unlock value for our customers. In this next phase of innovation, computing is more powerful and ubiquitous from the cloud to the edge. Artificial intelligence ("AI") capabilities are rapidly advancing, fueled by data and knowledge of the world. Physical and virtual worlds are coming together to create richer experiences that understand the context surrounding people, the things they use, the places they go, and their activities and relationships. A person's experience with technology spans a multitude of devices and has become increasingly more natural and multi-sensory with voice, ink, and gaze interactions.

The first two paragraphs of Microsoft's business description. From the 2018 Microsoft 10-K which is a part of the 2018 Annual Report. You can find it here: https://www.microsoft.com/en-us/annualreports/ar2018/annualreport

So right there I can see that Microsoft uses three segments. The way a business perceives its moving parts is crucial to understanding what they think is most important to their future. Reading through the Microsoft 10-K I can see that building on the "Intelligent Cloud

Platform" with Microsoft Azure, and innovating with AI are big parts of where the company sees its future opportunities.

Here is what I want to learn:

1. What is the heart of the business?

What is the company's main cash generator, *the heart of its business*? Most of the time this isn't going to be the same segment as what I'm looking for in #2, but it's very important to understand what the major cash generator is for the company. A company can't survive without its cash generator so it can develop high-growth areas, so determining the key risks are just as significant as determining the catalysts to the explosion of another segment. Let's take a look at Adobe, which is based in San Jose, California.

Here's how Adobe explains its business segments in the 2018 10-K[8]:

"Our business is organized into three reportable segments: Digital Media, Digital Experience, and Publishing..."

The flagship of our Digital Media business is Adobe Creative Cloud—a subscription service that allows members to use Adobe's creative products integrated with cloud-delivered services across desktop, web and mobile devices. Creative Cloud members can download and access the latest versions of our creative products such as Photoshop, Illustrator, Premiere Pro, Lightroom CC, InDesign, Adobe XD and many more creative applications. To expand our reach and improve the way we serve the needs of our customers, we create different combinations of these services, including our launch of a mobile photography offering that has brought new customers into our franchise and grown the amount of our photography subscriptions. In addition, members can access built-in templates to jumpstart designs and step-by-step tutorials to sharpen skills and get up to speed quickly. Through Creative Cloud, members can access online services to sync, store, and share files across users' machines, access marketplace, social and community-based features within our Adobe Stock and Behance services, and create apps and websites, all at affordable subscription pricing for cost-sensitive customers.

If you read through the description of the company's business segments it's going to be fairly obvious where it makes most of its money. The first line of managements description says "The flagship of our Digital Media business is Adobe Creative Cloud — so that's their cash cow.

As you can see, management explains that "The flagship of our Digital Media business is Adobe Creative Cloud—a subscription service that allows members to use Adobe's creative products integrated with cloud-delivered services across desktop, web and mobile devices. Creative Cloud members can download and access the latest versions of our creative products such as Photoshop, Illustrator, Premiere Pro, Lightroom CC, InDesign, Adobe XD and many more creative applications."

So, Creative Cloud is clearly the heart of Adobe's business, the cash cow, the way Adobe makes most of its money. Every company will likely have one core product, and your job is to figure out what it is, and any risks associated with it in the future.

It then goes on to explain a marketing segment called "Digital Experience" and also the "Publishing" segment, the former being a potential growth area, and the latter a legacy business — so it's clear that Adobe Creative Cloud is the heart of the business.

2. What is the major growth generator?

Often a company like Adobe has a cash cow like Creative Cloud that constantly generates fresh money, but what happens if growth slows for a monopoly product? Adobe can raise prices on Creative Cloud for so long, but what if new customer growth tapers off, and the only way to grow revenue is to raise prices? That's not a long-term growth strategy. I reading more of Adobe's 10-K I discover what I think must be Adobe's growth generator, or where they hope to explode their cash flow in the future: its called "Digital Experience."

In plain English, it looks to me like "Digital Experience" is Adobe's marketing segment. I got that from reading a block of text that explain the following. This is is in the very beginning of the Adobe 10-K:

"...businesses must determine how to best attract, engage, acquire and retain customers in a digital world where the reach and quality of experiences directly impact success. Delivering the best experience to a consumer at a given moment requires the right combination of data, insights and content. Executives are increasingly demanding solutions *that optimize their consumers' experiences and deliver the greatest return on marketing and IT spend so they can demonstrate the business impact of their programs using objective metrics.*

The description goes on to show that there is a new market (this suggests they are not yet well-established) and they plan to use data and analytics and artificial intelligence to drive growth in this segment. Keep in mind, this segment may work out well or it could be a failure. But as a possible investor, you are getting a much better picture of what's going on than someone who never flips through he 10-K.

"We believe there is a significant opportunity to address these challenges and help customers transform their businesses. The world's leading brands are increasingly steering their marketing, advertising, and development budgets toward digital experiences...Our Adobe Experience Cloud business targets this large and growing opportunity by providing comprehensive solutions that include analytics, targeting, advertising optimization, digital experience management, marketing automation and engagement, cross-channel campaign management, content management, asset management, audience management, premium video delivery, digital commerce enablement, order management, predictive intelligence and monetization."

So there you have it, I believe this is Adobe's "major growth generator" for the future. It's important that you understand that this represents potential future growth as distinct from the current "heart" of their business: Creative Cloud.

Sometimes management highlights their major growth segment, but sometimes you have to dig for it, and keep in mind that it might not exist. Why is it so important to have a growth area? Well, having a cash cow like Creative Cloud is terrific, but Adobe won't be a great future investment if the main segment is only growing 1% a year and you're planning on owning the stock for decades or more. You need to find catalysts that show how the company can innovate and grow.

When you're reading through segment information, there is

detail on segment growth. If sales (as a percent of the company's revenue) have moved up from the teens to twenties or thirties recently, you're probably looking at the growth generator.

3. What are the big risks for the "heart" and "growth generator"?

To find out about risks to a company's current business and future success let's keep things fresh by taking a look at a new 10-K, this one for Illumina, which is based in San Diego, Calfornia. Illumina is the global leader in genetic sequencing.

Even though Illumina is the 800 pound gorilla in the gene sequencing market, I can already see that competition is a serious threat to their business. The early text in the 10-K explains that genetic sequencing is a leading-edge technology, and scientific techniques are constantly being invented. It's possible that a competitor could come up with DNA sequencing systems that are better than what Illumina currently develops. Here's how they put it:

Although we believe that our products and services provide significant advantages over products and services currently available from other sources, we expect continued intense competition. Our competitors offer products and services for sequencing, SNP genotyping, gene expression, and molecular diagnostics markets. They include companies such as Affymetrix, Inc., Agilent Technologies, Inc., BGI, Pacific Biosciences of California, Inc., QIAGEN N.V., Roche Holding AG., and Thermo Fisher Scientific, Inc., among others. Some of these companies have or will have substantially greater financial, technical, research, and other resources than we do, along with larger, more established marketing, sales, distribution, and service organizations. In addition, they may have greater name recognition than we do in the markets we address, and in some cases a larger installed base of systems. We expect new competitors to emerge and the intensity of competition to increase. To compete effectively, we must scale our organization and infrastructure appropriately and demonstrate that our products have superior throughput, cost, and accuracy.

So consider yourself warned! Illumina may be the market leader right now, but in five or 10 years a lot can change. Illumina *could* be a good long-term holding, but this does not look like a "buy-once-and-forget-about-it" kind of investment. This is the kind of info you might not know as a casual observer, but when you dig into the 10-K you start getting a better picture of possible risks.

As I continue reading I find Item 1A that lists risk factors to the business.

ITEM 1A.   *Risk Factors.*

Our business is subject to various risks, including those described below. In addition to the other information included in this Form 10-K, the following issues could adversely affect our operating results or our stock price.

If we do not successfully manage the development, manufacturing, and launch of new products or services, including product transitions, our financial results could be adversely affected.

We face risks associated with launching new products and pre-announcing products and services when the products or services have not been fully developed or tested. In addition, we may experience difficulty in managing or forecasting customer reactions, purchasing decisions, or transition requirements or programs with respect to newly launched products (or products in development), which could adversely affect sales of our existing products. For instance, in January 2016 we announced an expansion to our sequencing instrument platforms, the MiniSeq system, and we previewed a new sequencing system currently under development that will deploy SBS chemistry on a semiconductor chip. If our products and services are not able to deliver the performance or results expected by our target markets or are not delivered on a timely basis, our reputation and credibility may suffer. If we encounter development challenges or discover errors in our products late in our development cycle, we may delay the product launch date. The expenses or losses associated with unsuccessful product development or launch activities or lack of market acceptance of our new products could adversely affect our business, financial condition, or results of operations.

When we introduce or announce new or enhanced products, we face numerous risks relating to product transitions, including the inability to accurately forecast demand (including with respect to our existing products), manage excess and obsolete inventories, address new or higher product cost structures, and manage different sales and support requirements due to the type or complexity of the new or enhanced products. Announcements of currently planned or other new products may cause customers to defer or stop purchasing our products until new products become available. Our failure to effectively manage product transitions or introductions could adversely affect our business, financial condition, or results of operations.

You can easily find the risk factors to the heart of the business and the major growth generator by reading through. Companies are very detailed in explaining all of the things that can go wrong.

This screenshot only the *start* of a long list of risk factors. As a potential investor you should be aware of them. I have listed the first four items below. If you want to read the entire list, you can find it in the Illumina 10-K[9].

- If we do not successfully manage the development, manufacturing, and launch of new products or services, including product transitions, our financial results could be adversely affected.
- Our success depends upon the continued emergence and growth of markets for analysis of genetic variation and biological function.
- We face intense competition, which could render our products obsolete, result in significant price reductions, or substantially limit the volume of products that we sell.
- Our continued growth is dependent on continuously developing and commercializing new products.

Also, the Illumina 10-K has a cool picture and "Genetics Primer[10]" with some background information about genes, nucleotide bases, gene expression, messenger RNA (mRNA) and protein synthesis. Come for the financial statements, stay for the biology lesson! There are some diagrams and clear explanations, so if you want to brush up on your biology education you can get a nice refresher course for free.

Keep in mind...this might seem like a lot of work, but it you want to do better than the average investor you're going to have to put in extra work. The best way to get what you want in life is to deserve it, and you're well on your way if you're willing to spend several hours of your life understanding a company before you invest.

Some business risks are the same for every company so you can just skim that part, but company-specific risks like the ones described above for Illumina can disclose important information you might not find anywhere else. Remember, you're an investigative reporter trying to turn over every stone, follow every lead, and learn as much as you can about a business. You want to find vulnerabilities, or things that could seriously hurt the company. A company where conditions have to be perfect may run into serious problems if anything unexpected happens. Compare this to a company that has a solid, dependable customer base and regular stream of income plus some new areas of growth.

Management will usually outline key risks in the 10-K, and that will be a good starting point to figure out what you need to investigate further after you're done reading. Watch some videos, read articles about the company, keep looking and learning. It's actually a lot of fun, and you will feel good becoming an expert having so much understanding about a company you once barely understood.

Properties

You can skim through this part, no big deal here because there are no big surprises. It's just a list of offices, warehouses, distribution centers, administrative offices, etc.

Commitments/Contingencies

This is where you'd find out if the company is involved in any litigation. This is not particularly important for many companies, but sometimes it's linked with the business risks section. If you're looking at an oil company then management might highlight a certain lawsuit related to a spill, and if it's a tobacco company they may discuss litigation related to smoking. You just want to make sure there are no lawsuits that could devastate the company.

ITEM 5. Market For Equity

This is really basic stuff, and if you're looking at the stock you already know the range that the stock has been trading at recently. If the company pays a dividend it's listed in this section. If the company has been buying back its own shares this will also be listed here.

. . .

Selected Financial Data

This is the first time you'll see the actual financial numbers that describe the performance of the business. It shows the financial highlights and lets you quickly see if the revenues are increasing or decreasing, it shows you the growth trends on important line items between the current and previous year on a number of specific line items, and gives you a bird's eye view of profit margins at the highest level.

I don't spend a lot of time on this section, but I think it makes sense to look it over to make sure nothing particularly horrible jumps out at you has happened like a huge one-time charge, a revenue shortfall, or a year where everything just sucked like an airplane toilet.

Management's Discussion and Analysis

Management's discussion, along with the footnotes to the financial statements themselves, are where the rubber meets the road when it comes to figuring out what's really happening with a business. I'll read this over and take notes and I recommend you do too. The earlier parts were a warm-up for this part, which is often referred to as MD&A.

Get a nice cup / mug / carafe of coffee and some chocolate chip cookies or peanut brittle to take your time reading through this part. This is where the CEO and their management team discuss in plain terms what happened during the fiscal year. This is where they talk about successes, failures, and any big and /or cool projects they have in the works.

Highlights from fiscal year 2018 compared with fiscal year 2017 included:

- Commercial cloud revenue, which primarily comprises Microsoft Office 365 commercial, Microsoft Azure, Microsoft Dynamics 365, and other cloud properties, increased 56% to $23.2 billion.
- Office Commercial revenue increased 11%, driven by Office 365 commercial revenue growth of 41%.
- Office Consumer revenue increased 11% and Office 365 consumer subscribers increased to 31.4 million.
- LinkedIn contributed revenue of $5.3 billion, driven by strong momentum across all business lines.
- Dynamics revenue increased 13%, driven by Dynamics 365 revenue growth of 65%.
- Server products and cloud services revenue increased 21%, driven by Azure revenue growth of 91%.
- Enterprise Services revenue increased 5%.
- Windows original equipment manufacturer licensing ("Windows OEM") revenue increased 5%, driven by OEM Pro revenue growth of 11%.
- Windows Commercial revenue increased 12%, driven by an increased volume of multi-year agreements.
- Gaming revenue increased 14%, driven by Xbox software and services revenue growth of 20%, mainly from third-party title strength.
- Microsoft Surface revenue increased 16%, driven by a higher mix of premium devices and an increase in volumes sold, due to the latest editions of Surface.
- Search advertising revenue, excluding traffic acquisition costs, increased 16%, driven by higher revenue per search and search volume.

Highlights from Management's Discussion and Analysis in the 2018 Microsoft 10-K.

Just glancing at the highlights above, it's clear that Microsoft had a stellar year, with commercial cloud revenue, which includes Microsoft Azure, increasing 56% to $23.2 billion. That's one hell of an increase.

Try to figure out what the important data is that the management team uses to assess performance, and accounting that you don't understand, and try to figure out how much cash the business has and whether it's wasting or losing money.

Earlier I mentioned how you want to think of yourself as an investigative reporter doing a story about the company. Well, as you read through this section just jot down any items that management explains that aren't clear to you, so you can ask "follow-up" questions to get clarification. This section will either leave you feeling unsettled or scared to invest in the company, or maybe it will make you feel confident that you understand the company's current trajectory and and have confidence on their future prospects.

Financial Statements and Notes to Financial Statements

If you're just starting out in investing then you've done really well to make it this far into a description of the 10-K. As you've figured out, this is high-level fluent discussion of all aspects of the business. I don't expect you to immediately have the skills of an accountant or financial analyst, but my hope is that you won't be scared of flipping through the 10-K and getting a lay of the land.

I spent many years not even taking a look beyond the letter from the CEO because everything else was in a foreign language. I simply didn't know what any of the numbers meant.

I think that you can be an outstanding investor without spending all of your life immersed in financial statements and 10-Ks. If that's all it took to get rich then every financial analyst would have a yacht and live the easy life instead of battling it out on conference calls to try and figure out if a company will beat earnings by a nickel or fall short. Remember what Charlie Munger said, "Most people calculate too much and think too little."

You can get so immersed in these 10-Ks and other numbers that you don't really understand what's going on. I think it makes a lot of sense to understand a company and visit the 10-K to fill in any gaps in your understanding rather than to try and figure out a company from it's financial statements because while they give you a strong sense of the company's financial health they don't always grasp where the company is going. That's something you can't always read about, it's something you need to piece together on your own — and the financial statements can help you find your way along the path, but they're not a complete treasure map.

If you are obsessive about tracking financial data you can go line item by line item through the financial statement to see if everything syncs up to what you read about in the Management's Discussion and Analysis (above).

The most important part of this section for you to examine (wearing your investigative reporter hat) is the Notes to the Financial Statements. This can seem like the longest and most detailed section, and it will give you answers to any investigative reporters question that you might have. Any remaining questions you will still need to answer, and you can Google for the answers, or even call the company's investor relations line and ask them to explain anything that doesn't make sense to you.

Follow-Up

After finishing up reading all the important parts of the 10-K you will be quite an expert on the financial side of the company. This will put you far ahead of most investors in the company who never took the time.

You may, hopefully you have some questions left over. Those questions can probably be answered with some online searches, but if you can't find what you need, just search for the company's name and "investor relations phone" and give them a call. There is a department at every company that handles calls from shareholders, analysts, journalists, and everyone else who wants information about the company. Give them a call and ask your question, just like a tenacious reporter working on deadline!

I know I've gone into detail here, but I always knew you could skim this chapter if necessary. I simply have never found a book or video out there that went through the 10-K and told me what to skim and where to focus my energy. My hope is that you now are no longer scared to at least take a look at this document, and if you've taken away one or three pieces of useful info then my job will have been a success. Like I said, even knowing what a 10-K is and how to flip through and read it will put you way ahead of most casual investors.

Think like an investigative reporter

Also, just to give you a visual of how to think of this process: Imagine yourself as an investigative reporter, and you've decided to do an in-depth article about a company. You want to be tough, but fair in your reporting, but you will have to dig for information, become an expert, and even talk to real-life people — either customers, or vendors, suppliers, or the company leaders. I am not saying that you actually have to call up and speak to investor relations, or write to the CEO, but if you were writing an article about a company you certainly would do that. I have personally written to the CEOs of three companies I've invested in, and I've received responses — in one case a typed letter in the mail, and in two others people at the company got in touch with me via email. My point is that I'm not sitting around just googling stuff. I get involved because my money is involved, and I truly believe that asking good questions and paying attention to the answers can put you in a whole different league as an investor.

I'm pretty sure that none, or very few of the people I know have written to a CEO. In fact, only one person I know wrote to a CEO and he never got an answer. I think it was because in his case the question (or suggestion) wasn't useful or relevant. If you write to someone and you have some crazy agenda you can't expect a reply. It would be like you replying to spam email offering to answer some crazy scammers' request.

Back to reality: I imagine most people in the United States has access to paper, a pen, a stamp and an envelope, and can write a thoughtful letter. The same could be said of writing an email to ask a question. I think the reason most people don't do this is that it requires coming up with a question, and believing the answer to that question is something you care about, and writing that question in a way that makes the recipient think it's worth their time to respond. Easy and quick to do in five minutes? No. Could it be done in one hour? Yes, I've done it. It can be done.

So the people who truly pull ahead in the world of investing spend the time to think deeply, form questions, and ask those questions of others to deepen their understanding. I can't tell you what should interest you, and what the questions are that you may have about some company that fascinates you.

I believe that reading the annual report and the 10-K will make your curious and perhaps leave you asking some questions. And as you search for the answers you will learn more and more and increase your expertise and fluency with all matters relating to the company, which in turn will make you a better investor.

FIFTEEN

GET READY TO BUY STOCKS

I WAS IN SANTA FE, New Mexico last week with my dad and on our last night in town we went to the Burrito Company for dinner. We were sitting in a booth and in the next booth over was a kid with his parents. We said hello when we sat down, but nothing after that.

As my dad and I were finishing up our dinner, the boy slid out of his booth and walked over to ours, flanked by his mother and father, who introduced us to their son Theo and told us that he had guessed my dad's age and wanted to see if he was right. So we said, "Sure, go for it." Right away, Theo said, "You're 13."

Theo was about 75 years off, but it didn't faze him at all. He was only six himself and he had a happy, relaxed, engaging presence. My dad asked him some questions about his family and Theo happily answered them all. When I asked him what his favorite food was he said, "Socks!" and then listed all the things that he puts on the socks he eats: ice cream, frosting, peanut butter, sprinkles, you name it. Some days he eats dirty socks, and sometimes clean. He was having so much fun recounting all the ways he prepares his socks; he had a vivid imagination to say the least.

We were all admiring this free spirit and his creative energy, and at that moment one question sprang to mind:

"How'd you get to be such a good kid?" I asked him.

"Because I'm ready," he said.

It was a spontaneous, unrehearsed answer that threw me off guard. Upon further reflection, though, it made sense. Theo was totally in the moment. There were no lines or lyrics or anything to remember, he's just 100% who he is and ready for whatever comes his way.

His attitude is such a winning way to approach life, always ready to handle whatever comes your way. The best way to do that is to accumulate as much wisdom as possible, and you can do that by reading.

Reading all the time will help you gain a better understanding of the world around you, and you'll start to see the patterns emerge that differentiate great companies from mediocre ones. This collage is comprised of 17 iPhone photos taken in a Barnes & Noble bookstore in Seattle. Shot, stitched, and colorized with the iPhone. Photo collage by Jeff Luke.

Get ready to pounce!

Reading and knowing a few companies really well will help you become a prepared investor. During good times when stocks are reaching new highs every day people forget that market crashes happen quickly. Being ready means that you know which stocks to buy, and you have cash ready to deploy. When the stock market falls quickly you may have the chance to buy stocks at a huge discount; sometimes these opportunities don't last long.

Therefore, if you spend some time getting ready for market declines, then you can patiently wait until a crash comes, or when there is a steep decline of 7% or 10% in a stock you understand. Once you have that bedrock of understanding done and you know the one, two, or three companies you want to buy, you'll be ready to pounce when they suddenly go on sale. Being decisive is much easier when you know what you're doing.

I would like to put some cash to work right now, but I'm waiting. I like to buy stocks, and I've put together a list of five that I like. I hope you've been doing the same, either on a list you've written down or that you're keeping in mind. Yet, as much as I want to buy stocks I simply cannot right now. The prices for all stocks I like seem expensive to me. But I can be ready.

New investors don't know what a crash feels like

It's very hard to describe what it's like. I think I got inoculated from the emotions that cause people to panic and do really stupid things when the market crashes. I say this only from experience, because as I just explained, I was buying stocks during the financial crisis when everyone else was freaking out.

For investors just starting out, you may never have seen a bear market or even a sharp stock market decline, so you don't know how you'll respond. I think the emotional response doesn't make any sense, it's like being in a sailboat with a friend, and suddenly it starts getting windy and the waves are smashing into the side of the boat, and you're taking in water. If you lose your mind and start to freak out you're not going to help yourself out of the messy situation.

Instead you can lower your sail (or sails if there's a jib or a spinnaker). You can make sure you're wearing your life vest in case you wind up overboard. You can get your flares out and shoot some off so other boats know you're in distress. You can get on your radio (every boat must have one) and call for other nearby boats asking for help. You can call the coastguard. I'm just pointing out a number of things you can do to avert devastation and ruin, and you can save yourself and put yourself in a good position to weather the storm.

The same thing happens when the market gets dark and gloomy and all the stocks you own, and every other stock in the exchange is cratering every day. Losses of 5%, 7%, 10%, 25%, and 30% are common when stocks crash. So you have to be philosophical about it, and realize that "this too shall pass."

The philosopher Spinoza said that "One must look at things in the aspect of eternity[1]." Always remember that you're buying stocks so you can benefit 10, 20, or 30 years from now — for you, and even for future generations of your family. So you shouldn't worry about the stock market storms today or tomorrow, because they will blow over and soon become distant memories. The long-term view will help keep you calm during the market's fluctuations, and this will help keep you focused on the long term.

SIXTEEN

HOW TO BUY STOCKS

MANY READERS already have brokerage accounts. If you don't you will need to set one up to buy or sell stocks, and I won't go through a list of available firms because readers can find this through a quick search.

I do believe it will help those investors who are just starting out to know there two ways to buy stocks that you should know about. To purchase stocks you must place a "buy order," and there are two ways you can do this: you can place a limit order or a market order.

I will describe both of these types of orders so readers can be well-informed about them[1]. If you've already traded stocks this will be very basic information, so feel free to skip over this chapter.

A buy limit order

A buy limit order is an order to buy a stock at a specific price or lower. For example, if you want to buy Stock X and it's currently selling at $77.50 and you want to buy it at $75 you would place a *limit order to buy* 10 shares of Stock X at $75. If the price goes down to that level your order can execute, meaning it is filled by the brokerage firm and you've bought 10 shares of stock at $75 per share for a total of $750 plus any brokerage commission. A limit order can only be filled if the stock's market price reaches the limit price. While limit orders do not guarantee execution, they help ensure that an investor does not pay more than a pre-determined price for a stock.[2]

Why would you use a limit order instead of the "default" which is called a market order? Well, during the trading day stock prices can fluctuate dramatically, and we're talking on a second by second basis. Sellers may dump (sell) a large amount of stock, driving the price down, and buyers may buy a lot of stock which sends the price up sharply.

Just as there are buy limit orders, there are sell limit orders as well, and they execute at the sell limit price or higher. While they're not guaranteed to execute, they're only filled if the stock's market price reaches the limit price. They help ensure that an investor sells their stock at a pre-determined price or higher.

Market order to buy

Let's say you wanted to buy stock X and its market price was $77.50. You would log onto your trading account, place a *market order to buy* 10 shares of Stock X. You don't specify a price, and you will simply get whatever price the stock is selling for at that moment. If there is strong demand when you're about to place your order then stock price might climb quickly and you'll see that your brokerage executed your order and bought 10 shares of Stock X at $81.00 per share for a total of $810 plus any brokerage commission. You paid the market price at the current market price.

There is nothing inherently wrong with placing market orders. One of the pros is that you get immediate execution at the current price, and it's guaranteed to execute so you don't have to worry that your order won't fill. One of the cons is that you lose control over the price you pay, and if you're buying a lot of stock market fluctuations can cause you to pay a high price if the market price suddenly jumps.

I've never had a problem using market orders, but I do wish I'd known about limit orders earlier. They give you a handle on the stock price and give you a degree of control. I've noticed that experienced traders tend to use limit orders because they've witnessed or experienced bad situations where the stock buyer paid much more than expected. The best I can do is share this information with you now so at least you'll know about them.

SEVENTEEN

WHEN DO YOU SELL?

WHEN DO YOU SELL?

I feel that a book that focuses only on buying stocks is not entirely complete, so I just want to mention that there are times when you may want to sell stock.

1. **You need the money:** This is fairly obvious, but if you don't have enough cash you might have to sell stock. I'd recommend keeping more cash on hand so you don't have to sell stocks to raise money, but sometimes you have no other choice.

2. **The reason you invested changed:** Maybe you invested in a company because they were innovating and growing in a way you liked, and for one reason or another the vision changed. If you no longer see the innovation you saw at the start, you may consider selling if you have a better opportunity.

. . .

3. **The leader you admired left the company:** The CEO who led the company may have possessed talent and integrity. They might have been decisive, and charismatic, and had a sense for the company. Without them, often a company will drift, and when it does, lookout! I've experienced this twice, and in both cases the departure of the CEO was the start of a long string of disappointments.

4. **The company has changed or lost its way:** Sometimes you invest when the sun is shining, and a few years later the clouds roll in, the company hits one problem after another, and then they spend more time fixing problems than moving forward. If the company is lost or in trouble, it may be time to sell.

5. **The industry is no longer promising:** Companies involved in clothing & textiles, furniture, sneakers, etc., in the US hit hard times when these products started to be produced in China and overseas. It's just the reality of the market that suddenly once good businesses become bad. What is a great industry at one time is horrible in another, so be prepared to sell stock if the whole industry hits the skids.

Okay, with that said, I think the best case is to buy stock in great companies and hold them forever. I hope you find companies like that so you don't have to keep checking them or worrying about what will happen next.

But, I think it's good to be aware that there are times when the story, main players, or industry changes, and when it does you are probably better making a change then holding on when things go from bad to worse.

EIGHTEEN

HOPE STOCKS WILL GET CHEAP

YOU SHOULD ROOT for stock prices to go down, not up. I know it's counter-intuitive, but think about it this way, if you're buying something, wouldn't you rather pay less for it than more? It doesn't matter if you're talking about sneakers or a car or groceries, you should always want to buy stuff cheaply.

When stocks get cheaper, that's always good news for a long-term investor. There are very few times when you should be bold, and if you look at the history of the stock market — those times are exactly when it seems you should be most afraid and sell everything.

It's crazy to sell stocks after they drop. Instead, you should either stay put and not worry, or if you have identified a stock (or stocks) that you've wanted to buy but held off because they were too expensive, say to yourself: "Today there's a bargain and I'm buying."

It makes sense to keep a list of companies you'd buy if the stock price got cheap. As you know from reading, I'm looking at companies like Bright Horizons, Stone Company, Zoom. I'm still adding to that list, and I continue to develop new ideas. I haven't bought them yet, but if any of those companies have short-term problems that crater the stock, or if the market gets the jitters, I'll be waiting for their stock prices to go down a lot.

During stock market declines, panics, free falls and breakouts that happen every few years, stocks will become cheap. You have to be the calm captain and maintain the right temperament to buy those stocks on your list that have become cheap. Everybody else will be running for the exits, and you'll be the one just walking in and buying solid merchandise at a good price.

In his book *One Up on Wall Street*[1], Peter Lynch has a a few bullet points toward the end of his book that make a lot of sense. I will include just a few of them, though there must be 30 of them in the book's last chapter.

- Sometime in the next month, year, or three years, the market will decline sharply.
- Market declines are great opportunities to buy stocks in companies you like. Corrections — Wall Street's definition of going down a lot — push outstanding companies to bargain prices.
- Companies don't grow for no reason, nor do fast browsers stay that way forever.
- You don't lose anything by not owning a successful stock, even if it's a tenbagger[2].
- A stock does not know you own it.

One of my favorite lines from the book is a great reminder that if you have some stocks that are winners, don't mess with them. Just let your winners run.

You won't improve your results by pulling out the flowers and watering the weeds.

PETER LYNCH

As a buyer of stocks you should root for prices go down, and your appetite for stocks should increase as their prices fall.

AFTERWORD

I hope that by now you've started making a list of companies you understand and want to learn more about. This will help you become a prepared investor, ready to be decisive when opportunities appear.

I'm a fan of writing things down, just to make a simple list, whether it's on paper or something you type on your computer or phone. It helps to get ideas out of your head, and for you to add to your notes. With actively writing things down it helps you to crystallize your thinking.

Be sure to take your time in understanding each company before you invest. The annual report, which you can download right away, or have sent to you by mail — is often the best place to gain firsthand knowledge about a company.

There isn't one single formula that will make you rich. So stop that kind of magical thinking right now. You need to get a grasp of the important concepts, know a lot about business and human behavior, and have the right temperament — one that doesn't seek action for action's sake, and isn't trying to get rich fast.

Experiment and enjoy

The only way to improve as an investor is to understand what you're doing and not be afraid of making mistakes. When you make the mistakes — and you will — just be sure to pick failure's pocket and learn something along the way.

You have unique life experiences that make you an expert in certain areas, and you'll have an enormous advantage if you stick to the businesses you understand. When you do have the occasional opportunities to buy the stock of a wonderful business run by a talented leader, that will be hog heaven day. Just be ready to pounce!

I hope this book helps you become a better investor. If you have any questions about this book or ideas for future editions, please reach out to me via email using the contact info on "connect" page that follows. I appreciate your time and look forward to hearing from you.

THANK YOU

This is a new book, and I hope you found it useful and learned something along the way.

Can I ask you for a quick favor?

If you can find a minute today to leave a short review, would you please leave one so future readers will know your experience?

You can leave a review for *No Bullsh*t Investing* here:

https://amzn.to/32oW46g

I appreciate your time, and I know people who are thinking of buying this book will too.

Jeff Luke

DEDICATION

This book is dedicated to my parents, Michael and Renee, for giving me so many opportunities in life, and also to my friends and colleagues for your encouragement. I appreciate you all.

CONNECT

If there's anything you wish you could learn about investing but didn't find in these pages, please send me a message and I'll consider including the material in a future edition.

Please connect by:

email jlukephoto@gmail.com

Instagram @jefftalksstocks

Twitter @jefftalksstocks

Thanks for taking the time to read this book.

I appreciate your time and look forward to hearing from you.

ACKNOWLEDGMENTS

I would like to thank the following people who helped bring this book to fruition. Edwin Paleoyaguar provided the artwork that graces the cover and the illustrations throughout the book.

Amadeus did exceptional work proofreading the first draft and made helpful observations that greatly improved the book. Any typos you may have found are probably the result of changes I made after he'd already done his work.

Liz Knueven was a helpful sounding board for ideas ranging from content to cover design, and has helped me get the word out about the book.

For those of you who encouraged me, looked at the book and offered suggestions on everything from the content to the cover, and to my readers who've told me that this book helps you — either in person or through an Amazon review — I appreciate you taking the time to let me know; it means a lot.

NOTES

Preface

1. Warren Buffett in the 1987 Berkshire Hathaway Shareholder Letter https://www.berkshirehathaway.com/letters/1987.html

Introduction

1. When I was a kid cartoons like Bugs Bunny, Road Runner, and Scooby Doo always seemed to feature someone stepping in quicksand: a loose, soggy combination of water and sand that can't support much weight so when you stand on it, it just sucks you into the bowels of the earth like an airplane toilet. Comedian John Mulaney said, "I always thought that quicksand was going to be a much bigger problem than it turned out to be. Because if you watch cartoons, quicksand is like the third biggest thing you have to worry about in adult life behind real sticks of dynamite and giant anvils falling on you from the sky. I used to sit around and think about what to do about quicksand. I never thought about how to handle real problems in adult life, I was never like 'Oh, what's it gonna be like when relatives ask to borrow money?' Now that I've gotten older, not only have I never stepped in quicksand—I've never even heard about it! No one's ever been like, 'Hey if you're coming to visit, take I-90 'cause I-95 has a little quicksand in the middle. Looks like regular sand, but then you're gonna start to sink into it.'"

2. What Is Financial Technology – Fintech?
   Financial technology (Fintech) is used to describe new tech that seeks to improve and automate the delivery and use of financial services. At its core, fintech is utilized to help companies, business owners and consumers better manage their financial operations, processes, and lives by utilizing specialized software and algorithms that are used on computers and, increasingly, smartphones. Fintech, the word, is a combination of "financial technology." From Investopedia https://www.investopedia.com/terms/f/fintech.asp

1. Unicorn Pimping

1. A **unicorn** is a privately held startup company valued at over \$1 billion https://en.wikipedia.org/wiki/Unicorn_(finance)

2. 15 Launched and Upcoming IPOs to Watch in 2019. NerdWallet https://www.nerdwallet.com/blog/investing/upcoming-ipos-to-watch-in-2019/

3. Why investors often buy IPOs https://www.fool.com/investing/2019/05/06/why-warren-buffett-wont-be-buying-the-uber-ipo.aspx

4. Scott Galloway has pretty good credentials and one of the experts worth listening to in the world of business, especially when it comes to branding, marketing and technology. Galloway, a Professor of Marketing at NYU Stern School of Business, and a general badass in online videos. This excerpt from "Section4" YouTube channel video titled: Robinhood, Apple's Rundle, Tesla's Valuation https://youtu.be/e7SMxpxjsjA

5. Blitzscaling: The Lightning-Fast Path to Building Massively Valuable Companies, Harper Collins uk, 2018

6. A unicorn is a privately held company that's valued at more than a billion dollars. In most cases these businesses have not even proven that they will ever be profitable, yet investors clamor to buy stock in their initial public offerings (IPOs).

7. A stampede of mythical proportions: The wave of unicorn IPOs reveals Silicon Valley's groupthink The Economist 17 April 2019 https://www.economist.com/briefing/2019/04/17/the-wave-of-unicorn-ipos-reveals-silicon-valleys-groupthink

8. Like many tech companies going public this year, Robinhood is still losing money. ... Though Robinhood co-CEO Baiju Bhatt has confirmed plans for their public debut, an exact date has not yet been revealed. https://www.cnbc.com/2019/04/11/ahead-of-ipo-buzz-robinhood-introduces-new-premium-trading-features.html

9. When you see the mention of the word "small investor" it has nothing to do with how many dollars are in your investing account. This term, along with "retail investor" are terms to distinguish between regular folks who have personal investing accounts, and enormous "institutional" investors who trade millions or billions on behalf of mutual funds, university endowments, pension funds and other institutions.

10.

11. Scott Galloway is a professor of marketing at NYU's Stern business school. https://www.youtube.com/watch?v=e7SMxpxjsjA

12. Peter Lynch is one of the most successful mutual fund managers. He ran the Fidelity Magellan fund between 1977 and 1990, Lynch averaged a 29.2% annual return, consistently more than doubling the S&P 500 market index and making it the best-performing mutual fund in the world. Wikipedia: https://en.wikipedia.org/wiki/Peter_Lynch

13. One Up on Wall Street by Peter Lynch - Simon & Schuster, 1989.

14. Unicorn Industrial Complex is a moniker I first heard Scott Galloway use to describe the multi-billion dollar companies that have fresh IPOs hitting the stock market, most of which have not yet earned a profit. Unicorns being the companies, and the industrial complex the investment banking firms and analysts that work to promote these companies in attempts to boost their stock prices to nosebleed levels.

15. I have gone to some of the annual meetings for companies whose stocks I own, but strictly for the formal sessions and Q&A. It never occurred to me to use these meetings as opportunities to develop useful contacts and learn about the business. Because of Lynch's advice, in the future I've decided to develop useful contacts at annual meetings.

16. Those born in the 90s may not even be familiar with the floppy disk except having an awareness of this mythological software item from times past. It's like the vinyl record or film photography, once the standard of the time and now a distant

memory. The floppy disk gave way to the CD-Rom, which was replaced by the DVD, which was eventually supplanted by cloud-based storage and streaming media.

2. Get 'Em When They're Little

1. Charlie Munger, "Sit On Your Ass Investing" http://jameslau88.com/charlie_munger_on_sit_on_your_ass_investing.htm
2. An **institutional investor** is an entity which pools money to purchase stocks, bonds , real estate, and other investment assets. They include banks, insurance companies, hedge funds, REITs, investment advisers, endowments and mutual funds. From Wikipedia: https://en.wikipedia.org/wiki/Institutional_investor
3. **Peter Lynch** is an American investor. Lynch was the manager of the Fidelity Magellan fund between 1977 and 1990. Lynch averaged a 29.2% annual return, consistently more than doubling the S&P 500 index and making it the best-performing mutual fund in the world. From Wikipedia: https://en.wikipedia.org/wiki/Peter_Lynch
4. Form S-1 is a document that the Securities and Exchange Commission (SEC) requires companies to file when offering its shares for sale to the public. Here is the Zoom S-1 https://www.sec.gov/Archives/edgar/data/1585521/000119312519083351/d642624ds1.htm
5. A unicorn is a privately held startup company valued at over $1 billion. https://en.wikipedia.org/wiki/Unicorn_(finance)
6. A fiscal year is a one year period that companies use for financial reporting and budgeting. The end of Zoom's fiscal year is January 31st.
7. https://medium.com/thrive-global/the-inspiring-backstory-of-eric-s-yuan-founder-and-ceo-of-zoom-98b7fab8cacc
8. Zoom CEO Eric Yuan on IPO: https://youtu.be/ja9VMe18sh8
9. I set up and tried Zoom for the first time on October 18, 2019. I was preparing this manuscript to go to press on Amazon, and I knew I should have personal experience using Zoom because I was explaining the company in such detail. There's nothing like trying something for yourself to truly understand how it works.
10. According to the company's regulatory filing Form S-1 https://www.sec.gov/Archives/edgar/data/1585521/000119312519083351/d642624ds1.htm
11. **Zoom, one of the most anticipated tech IPOs of the year, has one key profit driver: engineers in China, CNBC** https://www.cnbc.com/2019/03/26/zoom-key-profit-driver-ahead-of-ipo-engineers-in-china.html

3. Pay a Sensible Price

1. Market capitalization refers to the total dollar market value of a company's outstanding shares. Commonly referred to as "market cap," it is calculated by multiplying a company's shares outstanding by the current market price of one share. Definition from investopedia.

2. https://www.bloomberg.com/news/articles/2019-04-18/zoom-video-soars-to-16-billion-valuation-in-u-s-trading-debut
3. Zoom Video Communications closing stock price on September 20, 2019
4. There are 292,185,665 shares of Zoom outstanding as of September 5, 2019 https://investors.zoom.us/news-releases/news-release-details/zoom-video-communications-reports-second-quarter-results-fiscal
5. https://www.sec.gov/Archives/edgar/data/1585521/000119312519083351/d642624ds1.htm#toc642624_12
6. In finance, intrinsic value refers to the value of a company, stock, currency or product determined through fundamental analysis without reference to its market value. From Wikipedia https://en.wikipedia.org/wiki/Intrinsic_value_(finance)
7. A partial list of 2019 IPOs includes: Airbnb, Beyond Meat, Chewy, Lyft, Peloton, Pinterest, Robinhood, Slack, Uber and Zoom.
8. Another of tennis' little know truths is that tennis balls lose their bounce after playing with them once, and sneakers that protect your feet (and knees) cost about $140 a pair. Everything about tennis is pricey, which explains the country club feeling that surrounds the sport in many corners of the world.
9. This tennis racquet store is in Seattle, and located near an affluent neighborhood. This never caused the pricing for a "string job" to be that expensive in recent years, but the "Amazon effect" on prices is likely having some influence here, as well as the fact that Apple, Google, Facebook have recently come to town, which means there are more people who have the money to spend on a variety of things. The prices of most things from rents restaurants have risen steeply in price during the past three to five years in Seattle.
10. Warren Buffett, letter to shareholders from the 1987 Berkshire Hathaway Annual Report. https://www.berkshirehathaway.com/letters/1987.html

4. Design a Stock Portfolio

1. Charlie Munger on "Get 'em when they're little" investing: http://jameslau88.com/charlie_munger_on_sit_on_your_ass_investing.htm
2. Jeff Bezos: This is the one Amazon leadership principle that 'surprises people' the most: https://www.cnbc.com/2019/10/11/jeff-bezos-amazon-leadership-principle-that-surprises-people.html
3. Peter Lynch is an American investor and was manager of the Fidelity Magellan Fund. Between 1977 and 1990, Lynch averaged a 29.2% annual return, consistently more than doubling the S&P 500 market index and making it the best-performing mutual fund in the world: https://en.wikipedia.org/wiki/Peter_Lynch
4. "He was innovative, it was a new approach. Everything was experimental. Everything was new. Everything was exciting." —Edwin Schloss, speaking of Ben Graham, the father of value investing.
5. Jeff Bezos: 'We are the best place in the world to fail' Business Insider: https://www.businessinsider.com/amazon-ceo-jeff-bezos-best-place-in-the-world-to-fail-2016-4
6. Benjamin Graham is considered the father of value investing, and was the author of "The Intelligent Investor." Warren Buffett decided to go to Columbia Univer-

sity in New York so he could take Graham's class on investing, and Buffett credits Graham as one of the most important people in his life, next to his father. Wikipedia https://en.wikipedia.org/wiki/Benjamin_Graham

6. P - Profitable

1. https://finance.yahoo.com/quote/ZM/financials?p=ZM
2. https://finance.yahoo.com/quote/TWLO/financials?p=TWLO
3. https://finance.yahoo.com/quote/MDB/financials?p=MDB

8. L - Loyal Customers

1. Brand Keys Loyalty Leaders List 2017 http://brandkeys.com/wp-content/uploads/2017/10/Press-Release-2017-Loyalty-Leaders.pdf
2. Disclosure: I own Berkshire Hathaway stock, Berkshire owns GEICO and my car is insured by GEICO.

9. M - Moat

1. You can always sell your stock if the business begins to falter, but the problem is that sometimes an investor will not sell because a setback seems temporary, but leads to another small problem, and another, and eventually when the time comes to sell the stock is down some awful amount and it's never coming back. Ben Franklin said "Beware of expenses. A small leak will sink a great ship" and this applies to dwindling stock prices. Gradual declines in the value of a company translate — sometimes abruptly — into a lower stock price.
2. Data from Morningstar as of August 30, 2019
3. 8 of the top 10 Smartphones on the Planet Are Made by Apple: https://www.forbes.com/sites/johnkoetsier/2018/04/18/8-of-the-top-10-most-profitable-smartphones-on-the-planet-are-made-by-apple/#1beb9f67db18
4. A survey shows that iPhone customers are not even contemplating switching brands today. In a December 2018 survey by Kantar, 90% of U.S.-based iPhone users said they planned to remain loyal to future Apple devices. Apple CEO Tim Cook on the company's 2019 Q1 earnings https://www.imore.com/apple-earnings-q1-2019
5. Huawei's phone sales are ballooning while Apple and Samsung's slump https://www.theverge.com/circuitbreaker/2019/5/1/18525034/huawei-apple-samsung-smartphone-market-share-idc-2019
6. Jony Ive Wikipedia page: https://en.wikipedia.org/wiki/Jony_Ive
7. The only people I know who own Windows phones are people who work at Microsoft. I have zero friends who walk around with Windows phones except Microsoft employees who cannot use iPhones at work for obvious reasons, and are confined to using Windows phones for work, and are iPhone users only in the privacy of their own homes (with curtains drawn).

8. "The Four" by Scott Galloway - Portfolio, 2017

9. Galloway was featured on Recode Decode, hosted by Kara Swisher. Source: "What's the secret to Apple's brand? Boiled down to one word, it's sex." https://www.vox.com/2017/9/12/16290910/apple-event-iphone-x-branding-sex-scott-galloway-the-four-recode-decode-podcast-kara-swisher

10. Apple Users are Dumping iPhones and Buying Samsung https://www.zdnet.com/article/apple-users-are-dumping-iphones-and-buying-samsung/

11. Business Insider https://www.businessinsider.com/apple-iphone-more-loyal-android-chart-2017-5

12. Coke's Moat has More Fizz than Pepsi's" by Adam Fleck, Morningstar https://www.morningstar.com/articles/649012/cokes-moat-has-more-fizz-than-pepsis

13. Disclosure: I own shares of Berkshire Hathaway, and GEICO is a wholly-owned subsidiary of BH.

14. As of Q2 2018 only Samsung (21.0%) and Huawei (15.9%) had greater market share than Apple (12.1%) of the worldwide smartphone market. Smartphone Market Share https://www.idc.com/promo/smartphone-market-share/vendor

15. SNKRS app on Nike website https://news.nike.com/news/snkrs-app-update

16. Nike Has a New Digital Playbook—And It Starts With Sneakerheads

17. Sneaker makers like Nike and Adidas are facing a dilemma as resale is on its way to becoming a $6 billion business https://www.businessinsider.com/nike-adidas-role-sneaker-resale-market-2019-8

18. Nike vs. Adidas: The three stripes is making gains on the swoosh — but that doesn't tell the whole story https://business.financialpost.com/investing/trading-desk/nike-vs-adidas-the-three-stripes-is-making-gains-on-the-swoosh-but-that-doesnt-tell-the-whole-story

19. This is not a list of all wide-moat companies. It is a small group of companies that I understand well and I believe they possess wide moats. Disclosure: As of September 20, 2019 I own shares of Amazon, Berkshire Hathaway, and Waters.

20. The inside story of why Amazon bought PillPack in its effort to crack the $500 billion prescription market https://www.cnbc.com/2019/05/10/why-amazon-bought-pillpack-for-753-million-and-what-happens-next.html

21. Charlie Munger explains how Warren Buffett outperforms the market — 2019. YouTube video https://youtu.be/53vXIbsaBgw

10. S - Sensible Price

1. This process requires reading and work on your part. You can start with the company's annual report, and also read the company's financial reports. Watch videos about the company, talk to friends, go to stores, talk to people, do whatever it takes to get to know what the entire company would be worth to a hypothetical buyer.

2. At the time of writing, a deal has been announced in which Disney will buy a large part of Fox. The deal has not been finalized at the moment. For this reason I have not yet added Fox to the list of Disney assets, but by the time you read this this list of Disney's assets may include Fox. "Disney buys much of Fox in megamerger that will shake world of entertainment and media" The Washington Post by Stephen Zilchick December 14, 2017 https://www.

washingtonpost.com/news/business/wp/2017/12/14/disney-buys-much-of-fox-in-mega-merger-that-will-shake-world-of-entertainment-and-media/?utm_term=.06037bbdba3b

3. 3 Margin of safety is a principle of investing in which an investor buys stock only when the quoted price is far below the value of the shares. In other words, you only buy shares when the share price represents a discount to what you believe the company is worth (intrinsic value) on a "per share" basis. The difference between the intrinsic value and the quoted price is the margin of safety.

   For more information about the concept of margin of safety please see Chapter 20 of Benjamin Graham's book, "The Intelligent Investor" by Benjamin Graham, Harper & Brothers, 1949

4. Disney shares outstanding as of https://finance.yahoo.com/quote/DIS/key-statistics?ltr=1

5. Current price is $286.36 as of this writing on September 20, 2019

6. Data courtesy of GuruFocus.com

7. Seth Klarman means buying something at a high price, and then the price falling abruptly, and then having to wait for years for the price to reach the original purchase price. https://novelinvestor.com/seth-klarman-speculating-humility-cycles/

8. Timeless and Time-Tested Warren Buffett Watch Predictions https://www.cnbc.com/id/34206949

9. For those of you who'd like to watch it, the title is "How to Pay a Fair Price for a Stock" and the video goes through the simple steps to value the Starbucks company and a sensible stock price.

10. This is the closing stock price as of September 25, 2019.

11. Putting It All Together

1. https://en.wikipedia.org/wiki/Bright_Horizons

2. FY means "fiscal year" and it's the financial year. The annual report and 10-K will show the profits for the most recent year. Look for the line item that says "Net Income" as that is synonymous with profits.

3. Brazil's Stone IPO: more like Square than PagSeguro: 1. https://braziljournal.com/brazils-stone-ipo-more-like-square-than-pagseguro

4. Brazil's Stone IPO: more like Square than PagSeguro: 1. https://braziljournal.com/brazils-stone-ipo-more-like-square-than-pagseguro

12. The Magic Box

1. Charlie Munger quotes: http://www.quoteswise.com/charlie-munger-quotes-3.html

2. "How To Get Rich, Guaranteed," Scott Galloway https://www.youtube.com/watch?v=M53szMzppG8 Scott Galloway has several videos that I believe are "essential viewing." For anyone in high school or college or those entering the workforce for the first time I recommend "Prof Galloway's Career Advice"

https://www.youtube.com/watch?v=1T22QxTkPoM&t=97s and for everyone, "The Algebra of Happiness" https://www.youtube.com/watch?v= qMW6xgPgY4s&t=292s Galloway has a book by the same title, and it's a winner. I read the whole thing over a weekend (a couple of flights) and it's had a profound effect. I highly recommend this book for people at any stage of life.

13. How to Read an Annual Report

1. TPS report on Wikipedia: https://en.wikipedia.org/wiki/TPS_report
2. NVIDIA closing stock price on September 20, 2019 was 172.69 and

14. Anatomy and Dissection of a 10-K

1. Financial analysts, like any small group of specialists, have their own vocabulary, and calling this document the "K" is part of their verbal shorthand.
2. 10-K definition from The Strategic CFO: strategiccfo.com
3. Companies with more than $10 million in assets and a class of equity securities that is held by more than 2000 owners must file a 10-K. https://en.wikipedia.org/ wiki/Form_10-K
4. The annual report contains the 10-K, along with the letter to shareholders and other information about the business and its activities during the past year.
5. These analysts recommend stocks for their brokers to sell, so they're called "sell-side" analysts.
6. These analysts give recommendations about which stocks their institutions should buy, so they're called "buy-side" analysts.
7. As of market close on December 31, 2017
8. Adobe 2018 Form 10-K https://www.adobe.com/content/dam/acom/en/investor-relations/pdfs/ADBE-10K-FY18-FINAL-CERTIFIED.pdf
9. Item 1A of Illumina's 10-K lists risk factors https://www.sec.gov/Archives/edgar/ data/1110803/000111080316000175/fy201510-k.htm
10. Genetics Primer included at the beginning of the Illumina, Inc. 10-K https:// www.sec.gov/Archives/edgar/data/1110803/000111080316000175/fy201510-k.htm

15. Get Ready to Buy Stocks

1. Baruch Spinoza's "Sub specie aeternitatis" is an expression describing what is universally and eternally true, without any reference to or dependence upon the temporal portions of reality. From Wikipedia.

16. How to Buy Stocks

1. If readers have never before bought stocks, I recommend calling a brokerage firm for instructions, reading articles and watching YouTube videos to get a solid grasp of the basics. The limit order explained here is a relatively easy thing to do, but you should understand the basics of placing a stock trade before you get into the details of limit orders.
2. United States Securities and Exchange Commission (SEC) website - Limit Orders: https://www.sec.gov/fast-answers/answerslimithtm.html

18. Hope Stocks Will Get Cheap

1. One Up on Wall Street, by Peter Lynch. Fireside, 1989. This is an excellent book, one of my favorites on investing, and I think any investor will find the wisdom, based on years of experience running Fidelity Magellan fund, to be incredibly useful.
2. A tenbagger is Peter Lynch's term for a stock that increases 10x in value.

ABOUT THE AUTHOR

Jeff Luke lives and works as a photographer and writer in Seattle, Washington. His photography has appeared in *The New York Times* and other publications worldwide.

This is his third book about investing. Earlier books include *Stock Market Success* (2016), *Stock Market Intelligence* (2018), and Smart Stocks (2019).

His book "Animal Donut: Images & Stories" features artistic photos of animals & donuts: animaldonut.com and on Instagram @animaldonut

He enjoys biking, photography, writing, and taking huskies Maximus and Snowy for romps in the snow.

If you have any questions or would like to connect, please email jlukephoto@gmail.com